Vocabulary Explorations

Level B

Lesli J. Favor, Ph.D.

Steven L. Stern

AMSCO

Amsco School Publications, Inc.
315 Hudson Street, New York, N.Y. 10013

About the Authors

Lesli J. Favor

Lesli J. Favor holds a Ph.D. in English from the University of North Texas. After graduating, she was assistant professor of English at Sul Ross State University Rio Grande College, in southwest Texas. She left that position to write full-time for publishers of books for school classrooms and libraries. She is the author of twenty English/language arts and nonfiction texts, in addition to coauthoring this three-volume vocabulary series. She lives near Seattle with her husband, young son, two dogs, and horse.

Steven L. Stern

Steven L. Stern has more than 30 years of experience as a writer and textbook editor, developing a wide range of books, educational products, and informational materials for children and adults. He has written many test-preparation books and is the author of two novels as well as numerous articles and short stories. He has also worked as an English teacher, a lexicographer, and a writing consultant. Mr. Stern lives in New Jersey.

Reviewers:

Jessica Bennett, Language Arts Teacher, Brookpark Middle School, and Membership Co-Chair, Ohio Council of Teachers of English Language Arts, Columbus, Ohio

Elizabeth Henley, Language Arts Teacher, Ardsley Middle School, Ardsley, New York

Julia Shepherd, Language Arts and History Teacher, Arizona Middle School, Riverside, California

Cover Design: Nesbitt Graphics, Inc.
Text Design and Composition: Nesbitt Graphics, Inc.
Cartoons: Angela Martini

Please visit our Web site at: *www.amscopub.com*

When ordering this book, please specify:
either **R 056 W** *or* VOCABULARY EXPLORATIONS, LEVEL B

ISBN: 978-1-56765-193-5
NYC Item 56765-193-4

Contents

Note to Students   vii

Learning Words Through Prefixes   1

Vocabulary Mini-Lesson: All About Prefixes   2

Words to Know: Vocabulary Lists and Activities   4

  List 1   Words with Latin Prefixes   5
  List 2   Words with Latin Prefixes   10
  List 3   Words with Greek Prefixes   13
  List 4   Words with Anglo-Saxon Prefixes   16

Chapter Review Exercises   21

Chapter Extension Activities   23

Learning Words Through Suffixes   25

Vocabulary Mini-Lesson: All About Suffixes   26

Words to Know: Vocabulary Lists and Activities   28

  List 5   Words with Noun Suffixes   29
  List 6   Words with Verb Suffixes   33
  List 7   Words with Adjective Suffixes   38
  List 8   Words with Adverb Suffixes   42

Chapter Review Exercises   46

Chapter Extension Activities   48

Learning Words Through Roots   51

Vocabulary Mini-Lesson: All About Roots   52

Words to Know: Vocabulary Lists and Activities   54

  List 9   Words with Greek Roots   54
  List 10   Words with Latin Roots   57

Chapter Review Exercises   63

Chapter Extension Activities   65

Forming Words with Prefixes and Suffixes   67

Vocabulary Mini-Lesson: How to Add Prefixes
and Suffixes   68

Words to Know: Vocabulary Lists and Activities   71

List 11   Words with Multiple Parts   71
List 12   Words with Multiple Parts   76

Chapter Review Exercises   80

Chapter Extension Activities   82

Learning Words from Other Sources   85

Vocabulary Mini-Lesson: Words Come from Foreign
Languages   86

Words to Know: Vocabulary Lists and Activities   87

List 13   Words from Foreign Languages   87
List 14   Words from Foreign Languages   90

Vocabulary Mini-Lesson: Words Come
from Mythology   93

Words to Know: Vocabulary Lists and Activities   93

List 15   Words from Mythology   94

Vocabulary Mini-Lesson: Words Are Named After People
and Places   101

List 16   Words from the Names of People and Places   101

Chapter Review Exercises   107

Chapter Extension Activities   109

Learning New and Special Words 111

Vocabulary Mini-Lesson: How Our Language Expands   112

Words to Know: Vocabulary Lists and Activities   113

List 17 Technology and Science Words   113
List 18 New Words and Meanings   115

Words to Know: Vocabulary Lists and Activities   119

List 19 Medical Words   119
List 20 Legal Words   127

Chapter Review Exercises   130

Chapter Extension Activities   132

Learning Words from Context 135

Vocabulary Mini-Lesson: How to Use Context Clues   136

Words to Know: Vocabulary Lists and Activities   143

List 21 Words from a Nonfiction Text   144
List 22 Words from a Fiction Text   150
List 23 Words from a Science Text   156
List 24 Words from a History Text   161

Chapter Review Exercises   165

Chapter Extension Activities   168

Thinking About Different Word Meanings 171

Vocabulary Mini-Lesson: Understanding Words with More
than One Meaning 172

Words to Know: Vocabulary Lists and Activities 173

List 25 Words with Multiple Meanings 173
List 26 Words with Multiple Meanings 176

Vocabulary Mini-Lesson: Understanding Literal and
Figurative Uses of Words 180

Words to Know: Vocabulary Lists and Activities 182

List 27   Words Used Literally and Figuratively   182

List 28   Words Used Literally and Figuratively   185

Vocabulary Mini-Lesson: Using Descriptive Words with Specific Meanings 189

Words to Know: Vocabulary Lists and Activities 190

List 29   Words That Describe Physical Characteristics and Appearance   190

List 30   Words That Describe Personality, Character, or Mood   197

Chapter Review Exercises 201

Chapter Extension Activities 203

Understanding Shades of Meaning 205

Vocabulary Mini-Lesson: Words Have Feelings 206

Words to Know: Vocabulary Lists and Activities 207

List 31   Words with Positive and Negative Connotations   207

Vocabulary Mini-Lesson: Words Contain Messages 212

Words to Know: Vocabulary Lists and Activities 212

List 32   Words and Messages   212

Vocabulary Mini-Lesson: Words Carry Tone 217

Words to Know: Vocabulary Lists and Activities 217

List 33   Formal Words   217

Chapter Review Exercises 222

Chapter Extension Activities 224

Appendix A: Using a Dictionary   227
Appendix B: Dictionary Sources   228
Glossary   229
Index   239

Why and How to Use This Book

Why Vocabulary?

This book will help you expand your vocabulary and learn to think about words in different ways. But why is that important?

Having a strong vocabulary will help you communicate with people. Imagine that a friend asks you about your day. If you say that it was "fine," your friend will get a hint of what your day was like. But if you use a more specific word, like "routine," "tiring," or "fantastic," your friend will get a sharper picture of what you experienced. A larger vocabulary helps you communicate more clearly so that people can better understand your thoughts and ideas.

Using the right words also gives you power. If you want to write a successful job application or a convincing article or letter, choosing exact words will help your voice be heard.

The more words you know, the more you'll be able to read and understand in your daily life. You'll gain greater meaning from books, magazines, newspapers, and Web sites, and you'll develop a deeper understanding of issues in the world around you.

Increasing your vocabulary will improve your writing, reading, and speaking, in school and beyond. *Vocabulary Explorations* will help get you there.

About This Series

This is the second book of **Amsco's Vocabulary Program**, a complete line of vocabulary books for middle and high school students. In *Vocabulary Explorations*, **Levels A–C,** you'll awaken your knowledge of words. You'll study how words come into our language, how to figure out and understand meanings, and how to know which words to use. In *Vocabulary for the High School Student*, you'll sharpen your knowledge of word parts and increase your vocabulary. In *Vocabulary for the College-Bound Student*, you'll learn more challenging words that will help you tackle college-level readings and textbooks. Note that every book in The Amsco Vocabulary Program contains practice sections that will help you prepare for vocabulary questions on state tests and national tests like the PSAT, SAT, and ACT.

What's Inside This Book

Here in *Vocabulary Explorations, Level B* you will find a variety of lessons, features, and activities.

> **Sneak Peek: Preview the Lesson:** This quick activity will get you thinking about the topic of the mini-lesson.

> **Vocabulary Mini-Lessons:** These lessons introduce key vocabulary concepts and provide examples. The first lessons focus on word parts (prefixes, suffixes, roots) and building words. The next lessons explore the other ways words come into general use, crossing over from mythology, foreign languages, and technology into everyday speech and writing. In the last lessons, you'll focus on word meanings. How can you figure out the definitions of new words? What if a word has more than one meaning?

> **Words to Know: Lists and Activities:** In each chapter, you'll find two or more word lists. Each list contains five or ten vocabulary words and their meanings, as well as sample sentences. You're also given the pronunciation of each word (called the phonetic respelling because it helps you sound it out). After the word lists are three kinds of activities.

> > **Own It: Develop Your Word Understanding** helps you understand the meanings of the new words.

> > **Link It: Make Word-to-World Connections** has you make a personal connection to the words and learn how to use them in your own life.

> > **Master It: Use Words in Meaningful Ways** has you try using your new words in different ways.

> **Wrapping Up: Review What You've Learned.** This section summarizes what you've learned in the chapter.

> **Flaunt It: Show Your Word Understanding.** These exercises help you review the words in each chapter. The exercises will help you prepare for state and national tests.

> **Activities à la Carte: Extend Your Word Knowledge.** At the end of each chapter, you'll find these creative extension activities from which you or your teacher can choose. There's also an **ELL** option.

Oh, and one more thing. As you work through the book, you'll be greeted by **Word Master Mike**, who will use some of the vocabulary words to tell you about his own life. As he does so, you'll gain a better sense of how you, too, can use these words.

Hey,
I'm Word Master Mike. I love
learning new words and using them
to talk about stuff in school and in my life.
With a bigger vocabulary, I have more ways to
express myself. As you work through this book,
you'll get to know me better. I'll appear here
and there to talk about my life, using
new words from each chapter.
See you later!

This book is an important resource that will increase your knowledge and understanding of words. Continue with the rest of The Amsco Vocabulary Program, and you'll see big improvements in your ability to speak and write effectively.

Good luck!
Lesli J. Favor, Ph.D. and Steven L. Stern, *Authors*
Lauren Davis, *Editor*

Learning Words Through Prefixes

1

D o you know someone who can walk through a used clothes store, or take passed-down clothes from siblings or parents, and put together stunning outfits? Or someone who can take a junk car, add some new parts, and have the engine purring in no time? Some people have a knack for gathering parts and assembling them into a pleasing whole.

Words are no different. Many of them are made up of parts such as prefixes and roots. Once the parts are joined, the word's meaning is "whole," or complete. In this chapter, you'll examine **prefixes**, word parts added to the beginnings of base words or roots (main word parts). You'll learn a variety of common prefixes, and you'll add to your vocabulary a number of words that begin with these prefixes.

Objectives

In this chapter, you will learn

> What a prefix is
> How and why to add prefixes
> Words with Greek, Latin, and Anglo-Saxon prefixes

Sneak Peek: Preview the Lesson

Parts Department

The organizer at the top of the next page contains some of the prefixes, base words, and roots that you'll study in this lesson. How many words can you form using these word parts? (You may use each part in more than one word.) Spend five minutes in the "parts department" putting words together. Then share your results with your classmates.

Prefixes		Base Words and Roots		
con-	pre-	dict	cast	scope
dis-	micro-	respect	hale	phrase
in-	para-	chip	stop	able
non-	fore-	arm	vey	ject

Words Formed from the Parts Above

Vocabulary Mini-Lesson: All About Prefixes

Many words are made up of two or more parts. These parts may be prefixes or suffixes, base words or roots. You may already know these terms, but let's do a quick review:

> - A **base word** is a complete word to which you can add word parts. For example, *safely* and *unsafe* both contain the base word *safe*.

> - A **root** is a main word part on which words are built. A root is different from a base word because a root usually can not stand by itself. For example, *pedal*, *pedestrian*, and *centipede* all contain the Latin root *ped*, which means "foot." You'll learn more about roots in Chapter 3.

> - A **prefix** is a group of letters added to the beginning of a base word or root so as to create a new word. For example, adding the prefix *un-* to the base word *even* creates the word *uneven*.

> - A **suffix** is a group of letters added to the end of a base word or root so as to create a new word. For example, adding the suffix *-ly* to the base word *even* creates the word *evenly*. You'll learn more about suffixes in Chapter 2.

Forming Words with Prefixes

In this chapter we'll focus on prefixes—letters added to the beginning of a base or root—and how they form words. Like other word parts, every prefix has its own meaning. For example, the prefix *mis-* means "wrong" or "wrongly." What new words are created when you add *mis-* to the following base words?

PREFIX	+	BASE WORD	=	WORD
mis-	+	spell	=	*misspell*

  Emma <u>misspelled</u> the word.

PREFIX	+	BASE WORD	=	WORD
mis-	+	place	=	*misplace*

  Dad <u>misplaced</u> his car keys.

Now imagine that instead of adding *mis-*, you add the prefix *re-* to those same base words. The prefix *re-* means "back" or "again." What new words do you create?

PREFIX	+	BASE WORD	=	WORD
re-	+	spell	=	*respell*

  The teacher asked Matt to <u>respell</u> the word.

PREFIX	+	BASE WORD	=	WORD
re-	+	place	=	*replace*

  Dad <u>replaced</u> his car keys on the hook by the door.

By changing the prefix, you create new words.

  Prefixes are added to roots just as they are to base words. Let's look at a couple of examples.

  The root *vers* comes from Latin and means "to turn." The root *mit* also comes from Latin and means "to send." What words are formed by combining the prefix *re-* with these roots?

PREFIX	+	ROOT	=	WORD
re-	+	*vers(e)*	=	*reverse*
(turn)				

  The captain <u>reversed</u> course and headed back to shore.

PREFIX	+	ROOT	=	WORD
re-	+	*mit*	=	*remit*
(send)				

  Use this envelope to <u>remit</u> your payment.

Joining *re-* with the root *vers(e)* creates the word *reverse*, which literally means "to turn back." When a ship's captain "reverses course," the ship turns around and sails back in the other direction.

  Joining *re-* with *mit* forms the word *remit*, which literally means "to send back." To "remit payment" for a magazine you've subscribed to, you can send a check to the magazine publisher.

> ### Tip
> If you forget what a prefix is, think about movie previews. A *preview* comes before the movie; a *prefix* comes before a word.

Why Learn This?

Knowing some common prefixes can help you figure out the meanings of unfamiliar words. When you know a prefix, you have a key to unlocking the meaning of every word that begins with that prefix. For example, you may already know that the prefix *bi-* means "two." This will help you determine the meanings of many words, such as

> *bicycle*: a vehicle with two wheels
>
> *binoculars*: a viewing instrument for use with both eyes
>
> *biweekly*: occurring once every two weeks, as in *a biweekly meeting*
>
> *bimonthly*: occurring once every two months, as in *a bimonthly magazine*
>
> *bifocals*: eyeglasses designed to focus on both near and far distances

Knowing the meaning of *bi-* may not help you figure out *every* word with that prefix, but it will give you a good hint. For example, say that scientists classify an animal as a *biped*. Now that you know *bi-*, can you guess how many feet the animal has? (You may remember that the Latin root *ped* means "foot.")

Words to Know: Vocabulary Lists and Activities

Most prefixes in the English language come from Latin, Greek, or Anglo-Saxon (Old English). In the word lists you are about to study, you will see examples of all three.

Here are a few things to keep in mind:

> A prefix may have just one meaning (*bi-* means "two"), or it may have more than one (*re-* means "back" or "again").

> Two different prefixes can have the same meaning. For example, the Latin prefix *uni-*, as in *unicorn* (literally, "one horn"), and the Greek prefix *mono-*, as in *monocle* (eyeglass for one eye), both mean "one."

> Some prefixes are spelled in more than one way. For example, the prefix *com-* means "together," as in *combine*. The prefix may also be spelled *con-*, as in *construct*.

> Some words put two prefixes together. Your understanding of word parts will help you figure out the meaning of such words. For example, *reconnect* contains the prefixes *re-* and *con-*: *The electrician reconnected the wires after fixing the switch.*

List 1 — Words with Latin Prefixes

Study these Latin prefixes and the ten words that follow. Read each word, what it means, and how it's used.

Prefix	Meaning	Examples
a-, ab-	away from	avert, abrupt
com-, con-	together or with	compete, compromise, confer
de-	down or away	demolish, despise
dis-	not or the opposite of	disable, disrespect, distrust

Word	What It Means	How It's Used
avert *(v)* uh-VURT	to turn *away*; avoid	Jonathan *averted* his eyes from the awful sight.
abrupt *(adj)* uh-BRUHPT	sudden; unexpected (literally, "broken off")	The candidate's *abrupt* change in opinion puzzled her supporters.
compete *(v)* kump-PEET	to try to win or gain something that others want; be in rivalry *with*	Runners from around the world are *competing* in the race.
compromise *(n)* KOM-pruh-mize	settlement of a difference of opinion through agreement by both sides	Employees returned to work after they reached a *compromise* with the company about wages.
confer *(v)* kuhn-FUR	to consult *together* and compare views and opinions	My English teacher wanted to *confer* with each student about his or her essay topic.
demolish *(v)* di-MOL-ish	to tear *down*; destroy	Construction workers *demolished* the old building.
despise *(v)* di-SPIZE	to regard with strong negative feeling; scorn (literally, "to look *down* at")	Everyone *despised* the criminal for the harm he had done.

continued

disable *(v)* dis-AY-buhl	to make unable to act or operate	Engine failure *disabled* the bus.
disrespect *(n)* dis-ri-SPEKT	lack of respect	Jessica explained that she had meant no *disrespect* when she criticized her friend.
distrust *(v)* dis-TRUHST	to have no trust or confidence in	I *distrust* the claims that actors make in television commercials.

Own It: Develop Your Word Understanding

Prefix Wheels

Directions: Work with a partner to complete the activity. For each Prefix Wheel, complete these steps:

1. Fill in the Prefix Wheel by writing the meaning of each word in the space provided.

2. Complete each sentence printed beneath the wheel. Use your knowledge of the key word to decide how to complete the sentence.

3. In the blank section of the wheel, write additional words you know that begin with the given prefix or prefixes.

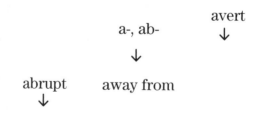

                                       avert
                     a-, ab-   ↓
                        ↓
   abrupt   away from
     ↓

Which should you **avert**: success or disaster? (circle one)

Are you more likely to speak **abruptly** if you're angry or if you're happy? (circle one)

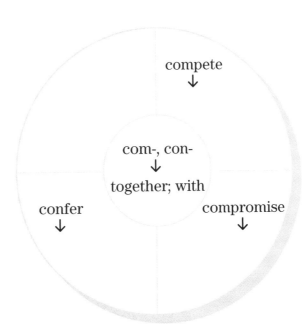

The last event in which you **competed** was _____

A **compromise** you made with a friend was _____

_____

A time you **conferred** with a parent, guardian, or teacher was

_____

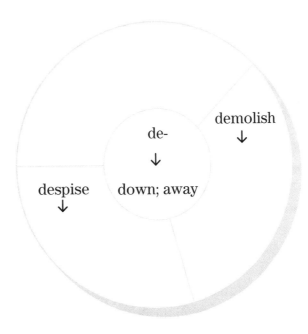

Which should be **demolished**, a rotting wood bridge or an ugly steel bridge? (circle one)

A food that you **despise** is _____

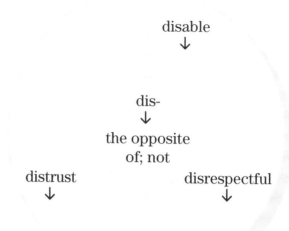

Which would more likely **disable** a bicycle, rust or a flat tire? (circle one)

Is **disrespect** usually linked to pleasant or unpleasant feelings? (circle one)

A person that you **distrust** is _____

Link It: Make Word-to-World Connections

Act Out in Class

Directions: In this activity, you and a partner will act out or demonstrate a word's meaning. For example, to act out the meaning of *distrust*, you might perform a short skit in which a person refuses to take candy from a stranger. Grab a partner and follow these steps:

1. Choose a word from the vocabulary list that you want to act out.

2. Spend about five minutes planning and practicing your act. Make sure that your act gives clues to the meaning of the vocabulary word *without* writing or stating the word directly. You are, however, free to use synonyms!

3. Act out your word for the class. Then let your classmates try to guess the word you acted out.

When my mom tried to **confer** with me about the fact that my room is always a mess, I **averted** my eyes from the moldy apple core on my desk and pretended I didn't know what she was talking about. I know she's right, but who has time to clean? I'm a busy guy.

Master It: Use Words in Meaningful Ways

Improving Sentences

Directions: Adding new words to your vocabulary helps you improve your writing. How? With precise words, you can make a wordy, awkward sentence clear and effective. Each sentence below is wordy, awkward, or both. Improve each sentence by rewriting the underlined part to include one of the vocabulary words.

averted a feud

Example: By apologizing, I <u>made sure a feud between us didn't happen</u>.

1. The boys decided to <u>try to win out over the other one</u> to see who could eat the most pie in sixty seconds.

2. I would like to <u>have a consultation</u> with my parents before I sign up to go on the field trip.

3. Sure, I tell white lies, but that's no reason to <u>decide not to believe anything I say</u>.

4. Everyone seems to love the new trend in straw hats, but I <u>have an incredibly strong dislike for it.</u>

5. When I pass my ex-best friend, I <u>turn my head so I don't have to see her with my eyes.</u>

6. Tired of the loud music, Mom <u>did something that made my music player not work anymore</u> by removing the batteries. (*Hint:* Add -*ed* to the vocabulary word.)

7. Since we each want to do something different, we should <u>agree to do neither one of those things but instead do a third thing</u> instead of arguing about it.

8. We were having a great conversation, but then Trent walked away <u>in a manner that was sudden and unexpected.</u> (*Hint:* Add -*ly* to the vocabulary word.)

9. Nobody likes to be treated with <u>an attitude that shows a lack of respect.</u>

10. My puppy found my sister's dollhouse and <u>tore down and destroyed</u> it. (*Hint:* Add -*ed* to the vocabulary word.)

List 2   Words with Latin Prefixes

Now learn four new Latin prefixes and words that are formed with them. Read each word, what it means, and how it's used.

Prefix	Meaning	Examples
in-	in or into	**in**hale, **in**ject, **in**scribe
non-	not or the opposite of	**non**essential, **non**stop
pre-	before	**pre**cede, **pre**dict, **pre**judice
uni-	one	**uni**son, **uni**te

Word	What It Means	How It's Used
inhale *(v)* in-HAYL	to draw *into* the lungs; breathe in	Smokers damage their lungs when they *inhale* cigarette smoke.
inject *(v)* in-JEKT	to force *into*, as by using a hypodermic needle	The doctor *injected* the baby with a vaccine to prevent illness.
inscribe *(v)* in-SKRIBE	to write, mark, or engrave (literally, "to write on")	The jeweler will *inscribe* your name on this bracelet.
nonessential *(adj)* non-uh-SEN-shuhl	*not* essential; unnecessary	To cut costs, the company was forced to let all *nonessential* employees go.
nonstop *(adv, adj)* NON-STOP	without a stop; *not* stopping	This airplane flies *nonstop* from New York to Los Angeles.
precede *(v)* pri-SEED	to go or come *before*	A flash of lightning often *precedes* the rumble of thunder.
predict *(v)* pri-DIKT	to say in advance; tell ahead of time (literally, "to say *before*")	Study hard, and I *predict* you will do well on the test.
prejudice *(n)* PREJ-uh-dis	judgment or opinion formed beforehand	The building owner has a *prejudice* against pets and won't allow them in the building.
unison *(n)* YOO-nuh-suhn	in agreement or at the same time (usually used with "in"—"in unison")	Our French teacher had the entire class recite the poem *in unison*.
unite *(v)* yoo-NITE	to combine to form *one*; join together	The colonies *united* to gain their independence from England.

Tip

Be on the lookout for new words created by adding common prefixes to familiar base words. For example, before a sports event, you might watch a *pregame* show. A movie or literary work about events that occur before those in another movie or work is known as a *prequel*. Such new words are added to our language every day.

Own It: Develop Your Word Understanding

Just Say It!

Directions: Work in a group of four people to complete the activity. Follow these steps:

1. Assign each person one of the prefixes used in the word list (*in-*, *non-*, *pre-*, or *uni-*).

2. On the front of an index card or sheet of paper, print your assigned prefix in large block letters. On the back, write each word from the word list (page 11) that uses the prefix.

3. Quietly, practice saying each of your words aloud. Think about ways to use each word to describe or tell about yourself. (For example, I have a *prejudice* against tarantulas as pets; however, some people think these spiders are delightful.)

4. Hold up your index card to show the group your prefix. Say the prefix aloud. Then read each of your words aloud. After reading each word, use it in an appropriate description or statement about yourself.

Link It: Make Word-to-World Connections

Rhythm

Directions: In this activity, you will work with classmates to create a rap, rhyme, or chant using some or all of the vocabulary words. Follow these steps:

1. Form groups of four people.

2. Choose a rhythmic pattern to use. Examples include a military cadence such as "I don't know what you've been told," the rhythm of a familiar rap, and the singsong pattern of a nursery rhyme such as "Twinkle, Twinkle, Little Star."

3. Play around with the vocabulary words, forming phrases or sentences and setting them to the rhythm. It's okay to be light-hearted and a little goofy—just make sure that your use of each word makes sense. Use as many of the vocabulary words as you can.

4. Perform your group's creation for the class.

Master It: Use Words in Meaningful Ways

Letter to the Editor

Directions: Have you seen or heard about situations in which adults seem prejudiced against people your age? Perhaps a store posts a sign saying, "No children under age 15 without a parent"— but there is no history of age-related trouble in the store. Or perhaps a neighbor complains to your parent that "those kids" shouldn't be hanging out in front of his house—even though you're doing nothing wrong.

Choose an issue related to **prejudice** and share your opinion in a letter to the editor of your school or local newspaper. A *letter to the editor* expresses a personal point of view, so include as many opinions as you want—just be sure to give reasons to support them. And one more thing: Use at least four of the List 2 vocabulary words in your letter!

List 3   Words with Greek Prefixes

You've studied two lists of Latin prefixes; now learn some common Greek prefixes. Study the prefixes and the words that follow. Read each word, what it means, and how it's used.

Prefix	Meaning	Examples
micro-	small	microchip, microscope
mon-, mono-	one	monarch, monopoly, monotonous
para-	beside, alongside	parallel, paraphrase, parasite
peri-	around	perimeter, periscope

Word	What It Means	How It's Used
microchip *(n)* MY-kroh-chip	a tiny electronic circuit used to process information, as in a computer or calculator	*Microchips* are a key part of modern electronic devices, from television sets to cell phones.
microscope *(n)* MY-kruh-skohp	an instrument for viewing tiny objects	The scientist used a *microscope* to study blood cells.
monarch *(n)* MAH-nerk	the ruler of a state, such as a king or queen (literally, "sole ruler")	Henry VIII was a 16th-century English *monarch*.

continued

monopoly *(n)* muh-NAH-puh-lee	control of a product or service by *one* person or company	If a country has only one telephone company, that company has a *monopoly* on phone service.
monotonous *(adj)* muh-NAH-tuh-nuhs	continuing in the same tone; not varying (literally, "one tone")	The speaker's *monotonous* voice bored the audience.
parallel *(adj)* PAR-uh-lel	extending in the same direction, at the same distance apart, so as never to meet	The rails of a train track are *parallel*.
paraphrase *(v)* PAR-uh-fraze	to restate in another way	The teacher *paraphrased* the difficult text in simpler words.
parasite *(n)* PAR-uh-site	an animal or plant living on another	Fleas are *parasites* that live on dogs and cats.
perimeter *(n)* puh-RIH-meh-ter	the outer boundary of an area (literally, "measure *around*")	Visitors strolled around the *perimeter* of the property.
periscope *(n)* PER-uh-skohp	an instrument for viewing objects not directly in the viewer's line of sight	A submarine's *periscope* enables the sailors on board to see above the surface of the water.

Own It: Develop Your Word Understanding

Prefix Matchup

Directions: In this activity, you will be given a prefix *or* a base word or root. Your job is to find a classmate who has the other half of your word. Here's how the activity works:

1. Your teacher will write each vocabulary word on an index card, then cut the cards in half so that the prefix is on one half, and the base word or root is on the other half. Finally, your teacher will jumble the cards together in a box.

2. Each student takes one card from the box.

3. Move around the classroom to find the person who has the other half of your word. When you find that person, practice saying the complete word aloud. Write the word (using correct spelling!) on a sheet of paper and review the word's meaning.

4. When everyone has found a word partner, share the results. One of you reads the word aloud to the class. The other person states the word's meaning.

Link It: Make Word-to-World Connections

Now and Later

Directions: In this activity, you'll think about words you're learning now and how these words may come in handy later. Pair up with a classmate and follow these steps:

1. One of you reads the first vocabulary word aloud. Together, make sure that you understand the meaning of the word.

2. On a sheet of paper, write the word. Then write an example of when or how you might use this word in the future.

3. Repeat steps 1 and 2 for each word in the list.

4. In a class discussion, share some of your results. Point out any words that you don't see yourself using in the future—and prepare to be surprised and informed by how others *do* plan to use the words!

> We had a guest speaker in biology class who was very <u>monotonous</u>. He went on and on in the same boring tone, using fancy science terms we didn't understand. Our teacher knew we were confused, so after the speaker left, he <u>paraphrased</u> everything the speaker said for us. Whew!

Master It: Use Words in Meaningful Ways

Did You Know?

Directions: In this activity, you will choose one vocabulary word to explore. Then you'll share a few facts about this word with your classmates. Follow these steps:

1. Review the list of vocabulary words and their meanings (pages 13–14). Choose a word that seems interesting to you.

2. Find *two or three* facts about the word that you can share with your class. For instance, what item in the classroom has a *microchip* in it? What is a country ruled by a *monarch*, and what is that monarch's name? Useful sources of information include textbooks, encyclopedias, user's manuals, knowledgeable people, and articles.

3. Write a few sentences stating two or three facts about the vocabulary word. Here are some phrases that you could use to begin the sentences:

   > Did you know that . . .

   > A surprising fact about (*vocabulary word*) is . . .

   > A question I had about (*vocabulary word*) was . . .

4. Practice reading your sentences aloud. Then read your sentences to your classmates.

List 4   Words with Anglo-Saxon Prefixes

You've looked at Latin and Greek prefixes; now study these four Anglo-Saxon prefixes and words that are formed with them. Read each word, what it means, and how it's used.

Prefix	Meaning	Examples
be-	to make; treat as; cause to be	**be**friend; **be**little
fore-	before; earlier	**fore**arm, **fore**cast, **fore**see
over-	too or too much	**over**confident, **over**crowded, **over**due
with-	against; from; away	**with**draw, **with**stand

Word	What It Means	How It's Used
befriend *(v)* bi-FREND	to act as a friend to	Josie *befriended* the new girl in class.
belittle *(v)* bi-LIT-l	to *cause* to seem less important; treat as unimportant	Jealous people sometimes *belittle* the accomplishments of others.
forearm *(n)* FAWR-arm	the part of the arm between the elbow and the wrist	Colin injured his *forearm* during the wrestling match.
forecast *(n)* FAWR-kast	an estimate of what will happen; prediction	Tomorrow's weather *forecast* calls for rain.
foresee *(v)* fawr-SEE	to see or know beforehand	Not even the political experts could have *foreseen* that the election would turn out this way.
overconfident *(adj)* OH-ver-KON-fi-duhnt	*too* confident or sure of oneself	I could have done better on the science test, but I guess I became *overconfident* and didn't study enough.
overcrowded *(adj)* OH-ver-KROU-did	*too* crowded	The theater lobby became so *overcrowded* that people lined up outside.
overdue *(adj)* oh-ver-DOO	past the time due or expected	Please return your *overdue* library books today, or you will be charged a late fee.
withdraw *(v)* with-DRAW	to take back; remove	After the agreement was signed, the president *withdrew* all troops from the country.
withstand *(v)* with-STAND	to oppose or resist; stand up against	The old wooden house could not *withstand* the powerful hurricane winds.

Once you've read the new words and meanings, turn the page to complete the practice activities.

Own It: Develop Your Word Understanding

Talking in Class

Directions: Work with a partner to complete the activity. Here's how it works:

1. Your teacher will assign you and your partner one word from the vocabulary list. You should then do three things:

   a. Identify the word's prefix and practice saying the word aloud.

   b. Express the word's meaning using your own words.

   c. Think of one other word (not in the vocabulary list) that uses the same prefix.

2. Your teacher will ask you and your partner to present your word to the class. You should do three things:

   a. Pronounce the word and state what the prefix is.

   b. Explain the word's meaning.

   c. Give an example of another word that uses the same prefix.

Link It: Make Word-to-World Connections

It's All in Your Head

Directions: Work with a partner to complete the activity. Here's what to do:

1. Read the headings in the table below.

2. Your partner will read each vocabulary word aloud. After you hear each word, write it in one of the columns in the table.

This word is completely new to me.	I have heard this word, but I've never used it.	I have used this word before.

3. Repeat step 2. This time, you read the words aloud to your partner.

4. Compare lists. Talk about when you have heard these words before and how you have used them. Read the words in the first column aloud to help them become more familiar.

Master It: Use Words in Meaningful Ways

Belittled in Boston

Directions: Advice columns are popular features of many magazines, newspapers, and Web sites. In this activity, you and a partner will create an advice column together. Here's what to do:

1. Decide on the name of your advice column. Examples are "Dear Freddie" and "Ask a Sports Nut."

2. Each of you writes a note to the columnist (Freddie or Sports Nut, for instance), asking for advice. Use at least one vocabulary word from List 4 and keep the note short—around 100 words. *Tip*: Letter writers may protect their privacy by signing their letters creatively, such as "Lonely in Dallas" or "Sad but Hopeful."

3. Exchange notes with your partner. Now take on the role of advice columnist. Write a note offering advice to the person who wrote in to your column. Use at least one vocabulary word from List 4, and keep the note to about 100 words.

4. Put together the advice column using the column's name and the letters to and from the columnist. Give a copy of your creation to your teacher, who will collect everyone's columns in a folder. When you have spare time in class, pull out an advice column and read it.

Wrapping Up: Review What You've Learned

Here's a brief summary of what you've studied in this chapter.

> A **base word** is a complete word to which word parts may be added. A **root** is a word part from which other words are formed. A root is different from a base word because a root usually cannot stand by itself.

> A **prefix** is a group of letters added to the *beginning* of a base word or root so as to create a new word. A **suffix** is a group of letters added to the *end* of a base word or root so as to create a new word.

> Most prefixes in the English language come from Latin, Greek, or Anglo-Saxon (Old English).

> A prefix may have just one meaning, or it may have more than one. Two different prefixes can have the same meaning.

> Some prefixes are spelled in more than one way.

> Recognizing prefixes and understanding their meaning can help you figure out the meaning of words. Knowing a prefix gives you a key to unlocking the meaning of every word that begins with that prefix.

> You've learned the following prefixes and words that contain them.

a-, ab- (away from)	micro- (small)
com-, con- (together or with)	mon-, mono- (one)
de- (down or away)	para- (beside, alongside)
dis- (not or the opposite of)	peri- (around)
in- (in or into)	be- (to make; treat as; cause to be)
non- (not or the opposite of)	fore- (before; earlier)
pre- (before)	over- (too or too much)
uni- (one)	with- (against; from; away)

Flaunt It: Show Your Word Understanding

In the following exercises, you'll demonstrate your understanding of each vocabulary word. You will use vocabulary words, or forms of the words, to complete sentences and to write sentences of your own.

A Word Bank

Directions: Choose a word from the box to complete each sentence. Write the word on the line provided. Each word may be used only once.

perimeter	demolish	belittle	disrespect	prejudice
distrust	confer	monotonous	microchip	periscope

1. You should _____ strangers on the Internet who ask for personal information about you, such as your address.

2. Laughing during the principal's speech was an act of _____, but I just couldn't help myself.

3. Quickly I built a sand castle on the beach, and just as quickly a wave rushed in to _____ it.

4. Mom had a _____ against graphic novels, but after I convinced her to read one, she discovered that she liked them.

5. Eating the same lunch every day can become _____ and that's why I usually trade food items with friends.

6. Please push all the desks up against the _____ of the classroom so that the middle of the room is completely open.

7. When a submarine must remain hidden underwater, sailors can view what is above the water by using a _____

8. Let me show you the _____ inside this electronic radio. It is this tiny square device next to those wires and other electronic parts.

9. Kelly is so insecure about herself that she tends to _____ her own accomplishments.

10. Sarah, Joe, and I met after class to _____ with one another about what we should do for our English class presentation.

B   Sentence Completion

Directions: Circle the letter of the word that best completes each sentence.

11. After watching the first half of the movie, I could _____ how it would probably end.

    a. predict   **b.** avert
    c. precede   **d.** inscribe

12. To save money for a bicycle, I have stopped spending money on _____ things like candy, fast food, and movie tickets.

    a. nonstop   **b.** overdue
    c. unison   **d.** nonessential

13. Coach Auburn was using white chalk to mark _____ yard lines on the football field.

    a. paraphrased   **b.** forecast
    c. parallel   **d.** abrupt

14. In my tiny town, Howard's Hobby Heaven has a _____ on hobby supplies such as model paint and airplane kits.

    a. compromise   **b.** compete
    c. parasite   **d.** monopoly

15. Numerous people wanted to _____ the new boy in our class because he was charming, fun, and fascinating.

    a. foresee   **b.** befriend
    c. withstand   **d.** withdraw

C   Writing

Directions: Follow the directions to write sentences using vocabulary words, or forms of the words. Use separate paper.

16. Use *despise* to tell something about yourself.

17. Use *disable* to tell about an accident.

18. Use *inhale* in a sentence about smog.

19. Use *inject* in a sentence about a nurse.

20. Use *microscope* to ask a question.

21. Use *unite* to make a suggestion or give a command.

22. Use *monarch* in a sentence that states a fact.

23. Use *overconfident* in a sentence that states an opinion.

24. Use *overcrowded* in a description of a place.

25. Use *forearm* in a description of a person.

Activities à la Carte: Extend Your Word Knowledge

The activities on this page are presented à la carte, like items on a restaurant menu, meaning that you can choose from a variety of options. Your teacher may assign an activity or let you pick the one that tempts your appetite. If time allows, you might do more than one activity. All of the activities feature the same ingredient: **prefixes**. Dig in!

Let's Get Jiggy

It's time to recycle that old jigsaw puzzle that's on the floor of your closet. First, put together some or all of the pieces. Then carefully turn the puzzle facedown, so you are looking at the blank backs of the pieces. On pairs of interlocking pieces, write word parts that form complete words. For example, write "be" on one piece and "friend" on a connecting piece. Write parts for about ten words on the pieces, then take them apart. Compete with friends to see who can reassemble the word parts fastest.

Notice Me!

Have you ever shopped for magazines? Chances are, you chose one with a cover headline that caught your eye. These headlines shout, "Notice me!" and bring in sales. With this in mind, create your own magazine cover on poster board. Choose a theme (sports, your favorite hobby, pets, etc.) and use magazine cutouts or your own art. Then write attention-grabbing headlines. The challenge? Use at least one prefix in each headline.

Alliteration Nonsense

A *nonsense verse* is a poem that is fun to read because it's silly, strange, or witty in unexpected ways. Write your own nonsense verse using vocabulary words from this chapter. To add *alliteration* to a line (a technique in which a writer uses two or more words that begin with the same letter), try using words with prefixes starting with the same letter. For example, a fun first line is "Microchips, microscopes, and monarchs—oh my!"

Memory Game

Create a memory card game. You need ten index cards and a list of five words that have prefixes. Use two cards per word—on one card, write the prefix; on the other card, write the base word or root. Shuffle the cards and place them facedown in rows. Invite one or two friends to play. To begin, turn over a card. Then turn over another card. If the two cards form a word, you get a point. If the cards don't form a word, turn them facedown again. Then the next person gets a turn.

Unite and Party

Use prefixes to lure friends to your house. How? Create a flyer to tempt them with a favorite activity—and use prefixes! For instance, you could write, "I **Fore**see a Party in Your Future" or "**Mono**poly and Mayhem—You're **in**vited!" Then write the details of when and where. Make copies of the flyer and give them to your closest friends. The fun is **over**due!

Parlez-vous français? ¿Hablas español?

Do you speak a language other than English? Compare the use of prefixes in that language to what you have learned about English prefixes. You could start by translating some of the vocabulary words in this chapter. Answer such questions as, Do the two languages use the same or similar prefixes? Does a word with a prefix in English translate to a word with or without a prefix in the other language?

Misbehaving with Words

Explore the value of prefixes by finding phrases and sentences in your everyday world to "misbehave" with. Look at signs, headlines, titles, menus, logos, and more. Remove, replace, or add prefixes and base words/roots to create new—and sometimes wacky—ideas. For example, a sign announcing, "Value Meals Available" becomes "Overvalued Meals Available." Read some of the "before" and "after" expressions to your class.

Learning Words Through Suffixes

2

Have you ever heard the expression "It's all in the details"? Explore the value of details by doing a quick experiment. First, glance at a person sitting near you. Then close your eyes and try to imagine *exactly* what he or she is wearing, down to the smallest detail. You may not remember details such as earrings or shoe color. However, you will remember the overall effect created by details working together as a whole.

The same is true of words—it's all in the details. When you read a word in a sentence, you may not notice all of its parts. However, you'll probably understand the meaning created by the parts working together as a whole. The "details," such as a suffix, are what create the overall meaning. In this chapter, you'll study suffixes and learn how they help determine the meanings of words.

Objectives

In this chapter, you will learn

> What a suffix is
> How and why to add suffixes
> Words with noun, verb, adjective, and adverb suffixes

Sneak Peek: Preview the Lesson

What I Know Already

Are you able to tell whether a word has a suffix? Test your suffix-recognition skills by sorting the words in the Word Box on the next page. (Remember, a suffix is a part added to the end of a word.) Write each word that has *no* suffix in the first column. Write each word that *does* have a suffix in the second column. In the third column, write additional words that you can think of that have suffixes.

After you finish this chapter, return to this Word Box. Make any necessary corrections using your new knowledge.

Word Box

brightness	forest	eagerly	pipeline
forget	they're	flatten	comical
backward	unrest	resistant	standardize

Words without Suffixes	Words with Suffixes	Other Words I Know with Suffixes

Vocabulary Mini-Lesson: All About Suffixes

As you learned in Chapter 1, while prefixes are word parts attached to the *beginning* of words, suffixes are word parts attached to the *end*. In this chapter, we'll take a close look at suffixes. Specifically, a **suffix** is a group of letters added to the end of a base word or root so as to create a new word.

Each suffix has its own meaning. For example, the suffix *-less* means "without." When you add *-less* to the following base words, what new words are formed?

BASE WORD	+	SUFFIX	=	WORD
color	+	*-less*	=	*colorless*

Water is a <u>colorless</u> liquid.

BASE WORD	+	SUFFIX	=	WORD
pain	+	*-less*	=	*painless*

Fixing my tooth proved to be <u>painless</u>.

The suffix *-ful* has the opposite meaning of *-less*. It means "full of" or "having." Let's add *-ful* to the same three base words. Now what words do you have?

BASE WORD	+	SUFFIX	=	WORD
color	+	*-ful*	=	*colorful*

The rainbow decorations are <u>colorful</u>.

BASE WORD	+	SUFFIX	=	WORD
pain	+	*-ful*	=	*painful*

Hitting my thumb with a hammer was <u>painful</u>.

You can see how adding different suffixes to the same base word creates new words with very different meanings.

Suffixes are similarly added to roots. For example, the suffix *-fy* means "to make." Let's add it to two Latin roots. Look at the new words that are formed:

ROOT	+	SUFFIX	=	WORD
forti(s) (strong)	+	*-fy*	=	*fortify* (*to make* strong)

The people built stone walls to <u>fortify</u> their village against attack.

satis (enough)	+	*-fy*	=	*satisfy* (*to make* enough)

Will eating an apple <u>satisfy</u> your hunger?

> ## Tip
>
> Keep in mind that many words have more than one suffix. Here are some examples.
>
> *helplessness* = help + *-less* + *-ness*
>
> *joyfully* = joy + *-ful* + *-ly*
>
> *dangerously* = danger + *-ous* + *-ly*
>
> What others can you think of?

Why Learn This?

Learning suffixes can help your reading comprehension. Suffixes often tell you a word's part of speech, and knowing a word's part of speech can help you understand a sentence you're reading. For example, words ending in the suffix *-ment* are usually nouns. Encourage<u>ment</u> and *amazement* are two examples. Similarly, many words ending in *-ly* are adverbs. *Hesitant<u>ly</u>* and *furious<u>ly</u>* are examples.

When you know a word's part of speech, you can see how the word relates to other words in the sentence. This helps you understand the sentence better. Look at these examples:

Mr. Jackson felt *confident* as he began his speech.

(*Confident* is an adjective, describing Mr. Jackson's feeling.)

Mr. Jackson smiled *confidently* as he began his speech.

(*Confidently* is an adverb, describing how Mr. Jackson was smiling.)

Even if you didn't know what *confidently* means, you could use your knowledge of the suffix *-ly* to figure out that it's an adverb describing how Mr. Jackson smiled. This gives you a clue about what it must mean.

Quick Review: The Parts of Speech

Suffixes help you identify these parts of speech:

Noun   Names a person place, thing, or idea.
Examples: *emperor, nation, train, peace*

Verb   Expresses action or state of being.
Examples: *throw, speak, memorize*

Adjective   Describes a noun or a pronoun.
Examples: *wide, red, noisy*

Adverb   Describes a verb, adjective, or another adverb.
Examples: *rapidly, accurately*

ords to Know: Vocabulary Lists and Activities

In Chapter 1, prefixes were grouped according to their language of origin: Latin, Greek, or Anglo-Saxon. Suffixes, too, come from different languages, and many English words combine suffixes from one language with roots and prefixes from other languages. Rather than focus on their origin, however, this chapter groups suffixes by the part of speech they usually show: noun, verb, adjective, and adverb.

Just as with prefixes, keep several things in mind:

> A suffix may have more than one meaning. For example, the noun suffix *-tion* can refer to an "action" or to a "condition." Compare these sentences:

The pounding waves caused *erosion* of the beach.

(the *action* of wearing away)

Street signs can cause *confusion* for foreign visitors.

(the *condition* of being confused)

> Two different suffixes can have the same meaning. For example, the suffixes *-or* and *-ist* both mean "person who," as in *narrator* and *bicyclist.*

> Adding a suffix can change a word from one part of speech to another.

From verb to noun: amuse + -*ment* = amusement
From adjective to verb: tight + -*en* = tighten
From noun to adjective: motion + -*less* = motionless
From adjective to adverb: gradual + -*ly* = gradually

> Some suffixes are spelled in more than one way. For example, -*able* and -*ible* are two forms of the same suffix, meaning "capable of being," as in *breakable* and *divisible*.

> When a suffix is added to a base word, the word may stay the same, or letters may be dropped, added, or changed. Here are a few examples:

doubt + -*ful* = doubt*ful*   (no spelling change)

believe + -*able* = believ*able*   (the *e* is dropped)

merry + -*ly* = merri*ly*   (*y* changes to *i*)

You'll learn more about such spelling changes in Chapter 4.

List 5   Words with Noun Suffixes

Here are four suffixes that form nouns—names of people, places, things, or ideas. Study the suffixes and the ten words (nouns) that follow. Read each word, what it means, and how it's used.

Suffix	Meaning	Examples
-age	condition of	marri**age**, short**age**
-cy	quality, condition, or fact of being	accura**cy**, freque**ncy**, secre**cy**
-ity, -ty	quality, condition, or fact of being	loyal**ty**, maturi**ty**, uni**ty**
-ness	quality or condition of being	clums**iness**, conscious**ness**

Word	What It Means	How It's Used
marriage *(n)* MAR-ij	*condition of* being married	The Stegers had a party to celebrate their twenty years of *marriage*.
shortage *(n)* SHAWR-tij	*condition of* not having enough; lack	Some hospitals are experiencing a *shortage* of nurses.
accuracy *(n)* AK-yer-uh-see	*quality of being* accurate; correctness	Please check your application form for *accuracy* before you hand it in.
frequency *(n)* FREE-kwuhn-see	*fact of being* frequent; occurring often	I can tell you love art by the *frequency* of your visits to the museum.
secrecy *(n)* SEE-kruh-see	*condition of being* secret	The plot to overthrow the king was carried out in *secrecy*.
loyalty *(n)* LOI-uhl-tee	*fact of being* loyal	Mandy would never question the *loyalty* of her closest friend.
maturity *(n)* muh-CHOOR-i-tee	*quality of being* mature	Young Carlos shows surprising *maturity* in the way he plays the violin.
unity *(n)* YOO-ni-tee	*condition of being* one, or united (See *uni-* on page 10.)	National *unity* helps a country survive the effects of war.
clumsiness *(n)* KLUHM-zee-nis	*quality of being* clumsy	My sister laughs at my *clumsiness;* I trip over everything.
consciousness *(n)* KON-shuhs-nis	*condition of being* conscious	Nicole fainted from the heat, but she quickly regained *consciousness*.

Own It: Develop Your Word Understanding

Suffix Organizers

Directions: Work with a partner to complete the activity. Each of you completes two of the four organizers that follow. Then share your results. For each organizer, follow these steps:

1. *Top:* Read the suffix or suffixes printed in the top box.
2. *Middle:* In the "used in" box, write the vocabulary words that use the given suffix(es). In the "meaning" box, write the meaning of the suffix(es). In the "memory cue" box, sketch or write a clue to help you remember the suffix's meaning.
3. *Bottom:* Use your knowledge of each key word to complete the sentences.

-age

| used in | meaning | memory cue |

Two people in a celebrity *marriage* are _____

_____

Opening my kitchen cupboard, I noticed a *shortage* of _____

_____

-cy

| used in | meaning | memory cue |

Accuracy is important when a teacher _____

_____

Something that I eat with great *frequency* is _____

An activity that requires *secrecy* is _____

-ity, -ty

used in   meaning   memory cue

I feel *loyalty* toward _____

A way of showing *maturity* in behavior is to _____

I feel a sense of *unity* with _____

-ness

used in   meaning   memory cue

I had to laugh at my *clumsiness* when I _____

The athlete lost *consciousness* when _____

Link It: Make Word-to-World Connections

All About Us

Directions: Your assignment is to create a poster about your family or your "family" of friends. Here's what you need to do:

1. Study the list of vocabulary words. Think about ways these words connect to you and your family or friends. Perhaps you can use the words to *inform* (give information), to *entertain* (tell amusing facts or stories), to *describe* (give details to create a mental image), or to *persuade* (convince readers to share your view of your family). Write phrases and sentences using the vocabulary words.

2. Add some visual appeal. Gather art supplies, photographs, mementos, and other materials to make your poster "pop."

3. Put it all together. Arrange the sentences and phrases from step 1 on the poster and use the materials from step 2 to make the project eye-catching.

4. Share your poster with your family, friends, and classmates.

Master It: Use Words in Meaningful Ways

Abstract Exhibit

Directions: Each noun in the vocabulary list is an *abstract noun*. This means you can't touch it, taste it, smell it, or use other senses to experience it.

Even though the nouns are abstract, you probably have mental images linked to them. For example, the word *marriage* may make you picture your parents. *Unity* may bring to mind a photograph of your basketball team. These mental images help you make sense of abstract nouns.

In this activity, you'll explore one abstract noun. Follow these four steps:

1. Review the vocabulary words, thinking about mental images that they inspire. Choose one word for this project.

2. Write a paragraph describing the image that the key word brings to mind. For a powerful paragraph, give details that appeal to the various senses (touch, taste, smell, hearing, sight).

3. Find or create a picture that is the same as or similar to the mental image you described in step 2.

4. On paper or poster board, attach the picture and the paragraph. Display your project in class during an Abstract Exhibit.

List 6   Words with Verb Suffixes

In the last list, you learned suffixes that form nouns—people, places, things, or ideas. Now you'll learn suffixes that form verbs—words that express action or a state of being. Study the suffixes and the words (verbs) that follow. Read each word, what it means, and how it's used.

Suffix	Meaning	Examples
-ate	to make	allevi**ate**, liber**ate**
-en	to make	broad**en**, height**en**
-fy	to make	beauti**fy**, clari**fy**, simpli**fy**
-ize	to make	computer**ize**, familia**rize**, standard**ize**

Word	What It Means	How It's Used
alleviate *(v)* uh-LEE-vee-ate	to lessen or relieve	Having a good friend to turn to helped *alleviate* some of her suffering.
liberate *(v)* LIH-buh-rayt	*to make* or set free (from Latin *liber*, meaning "free")	Soldiers entered the village and *liberated* the prisoners.
broaden *(v)* BRAWD-n	*to make* more wide; expand	You can *broaden* you knowledge by reading a wide range of books.
heighten *(v)* HIGH-tn	*to make* more intense; enhance	Creepy music *heightens* the suspense in a horror movie.
beautify *(v)* BYOO-tuh-fie	*to make* beautiful	Mom planted colorful flowers to *beautify* the front yard.
clarify *(v)* KLAR-uh-fie	*to make* clear; explain	Reporters asked the candidate to *clarify* his views on the proposed highway.
simplify *(v)* SIM-pluh-fie	*to make* simple	Jamie *simplified* the instructions for her younger brother.
computerize *(v)* kuhm-PYOO-tuh-rize	to operate or control by means of computers	The company spent millions of dollars to *computerize* its machinery.
familiarize *(v)* fuh-MIL-yuh-rize	*to make* familiar or acquainted	Before trying to operate this device, you should *familiarize* yourself with the control buttons.
standardize *(v)* STAN-der-dize	*to make* standard	*Standardizing* the size of the boxes enabled the manufacturer to speed up production and cut costs.

Own It: Develop Your Word Understanding

Suffix Wheels

Directions: Follow the steps to complete the activity.

1. Fill in the four Suffix Wheels by writing the meaning of each word in the space provided.

2. In each empty section of a wheel, write an additional word that uses the given suffix, along with the meaning of the word.

3. Your teacher will call out someone's name and identify a suffix. That person reads one section in that Suffix Wheel. Then that person calls out someone else's name and identifies a suffix.

4. Continue calling out names and reading sections from the wheels until each wheel has been read completely.

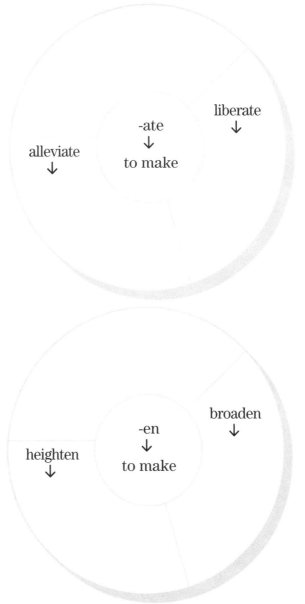

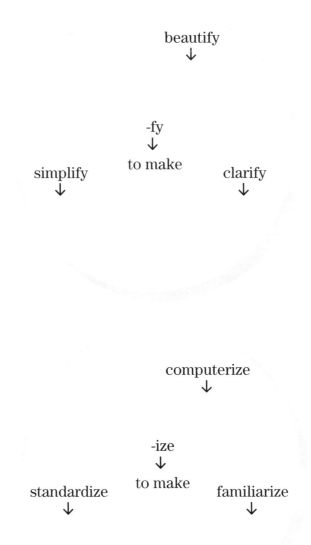

beautify
↓

-fy
↓
to make

simplify   clarify
↓   ↓

computerize
↓

-ize
↓
to make

standardize   familiarize
↓   ↓

Link It: Make Word-to-World Connections

Let Me Explain

Directions: Can you explain how to *computerize* your teacher's grade book? Or how to *beautify* the ugly brick wall along the side of the school? Think about how the verbs in the vocabulary list relate to something you know how to do. Then follow these steps:

1. Write a few sentences that explain how to do something. You can be serious or funny. You can explain something that your friends know little about, or something that is familiar to many. The goal is to use *two or more* vocabulary words in your explanation.

2. Gather in small groups. Read your explanation aloud. Then ask group members to identify the vocabulary words used in your explanation. Ask them if they can suggest yet another vocabulary word that would fit in your explanation.

Our phys. ed. teacher spent a lot of time <u>familiarizing</u> us with the rules of kickball. He <u>clarified</u> every single rule. By the time he was done, there was barely any time left to play! The next time, I wish he would <u>simplify</u> things and give us a shorter talk.

Master It: Use Words in Meaningful Ways

Goods and Services

Directions: A key way to earn money is to sell goods or services. Examples of "goods" are cookies, shirts, and music CDs. "Services," on the other hand, include haircuts, car washes, and tutoring. In a class discussion, identify goods and services that may be purchased in your community. Then follow these steps to complete the activity:

1. Skim the vocabulary words (page 34), asking, "Does this word inspire me with an idea for selling a good or service?" Jot down your ideas.

2. Choose the strongest idea you recorded in step 1. Then write a plan of action telling how you could make money by selling this good or service. In your plan, use one or more vocabulary words.

3. Give a copy of your plan to your teacher, who will place all the plans in a Goods and Services folder. When you have spare time in class, pull out a money-making plan and read it. Who knows, you may put some of these plans into action!

List 7   Words with Adjective Suffixes

The following suffixes are used to form adjectives—words that describe nouns. Learn these common suffixes and ten words (adjectives) that are formed with them. Read each word, what it means, and how it's used.

Suffix	Meaning	Examples
-al	of, suitable for, or relating to	fictional, theatrical
-ant, -ent	being or acting in a certain way	defiant, dependent, persistent
-ic, -ical	like, relating to, or having the qualities of	angelic, biographical
-ive	relating to or inclined to	appreciative, competitive, descriptive

Word	What It Means	How It's Used
fictional *(adj)* FIK-shuh-nuhl	*of* fiction; imagined	The detective is a *fictional* character loosely based on the author's husband.
theatrical *(adj)* thee-A-tri-kuhl	*of or relating to* the theater	The actor's finest *theatrical* performance was in the role of Hamlet.
defiant *(adj)* di-FIE-uhnt	openly resisting; bold	Emily's *defiant* refusal to help with the chores made her brother angry.
dependent *(adj)* di-PEN-duhnt	relying on another for support or care	Babies are *dependent* on their parents.
persistent *(adj)* per-SIS-tuhnt	not giving up; determined	Hannah was *persistent* in her efforts to make the debating team.
angelic *(adj)* an-JEH-lik	*like or having the qualities of* an angel	Tommy was often a little devil at home, but the kindergarten teacher praised him for his *angelic* behavior.

continued

biographical *(adj)* bie-uh-GRAF-i-kuhl	*relating to* a person's life	Kayla wrote a *biographical* report about Helen Keller.
appreciative *(adj)* uh-PREE-shuh-tiv	feeling or showing appreciation; grateful	The *appreciative* audience cheered as the actors took their bows.
competitive *(adj)* kuhm-PEH-ti-tiv	involving or based on the efforts of people who are competing (See *compete* on Word List 1, page 00.)	To succeed in *competitive* sports, athletes must train.
descriptive *(adj)* di-SKRIP-tiv	that describes	Authors use *descriptive* details to bring their writing to life.

Own It: Develop Your Word Understanding

Suffix Matchup

Directions: Each vocabulary word combines a *root* and a *suffix*. Some, but not all, of the roots change their spelling when the suffix is added. (For example, in *defy*, the *y* changes to *i* when *-ant* is added, forming *defiant*.)

In this activity, you will be given a root *or* a suffix. Your job is to find a classmate who has the other half of your word. Follow these steps:

1. Your teacher will break each vocabulary word into a root and a suffix. He or she will write each part on separate index cards. All the cards will be jumbled together in a box.

2. Each student chooses one card from the box.

3. Move around the classroom to find the person who has the other half of your vocabulary word. When you find that person, practice saying the complete word aloud. Write the word (using correct spelling!) on a sheet of paper and review the word's meaning.

4. When everyone has found a word partner, share the results. One of you reads the word aloud and shows how the root and the suffix are combined. The other person states the word's meaning.

Our English teacher had us do a <u>theatrical</u> performance of the play, *Romeo and Juliet.* My <u>angelic</u> crush Emily played the part of Juliet, and Joe, the class jerk, got the part of Romeo. I was so jealous. And Joe was <u>persistent</u> about bragging to everyone that he got the lead. I wasn't <u>appreciative</u> of that!

Link It: Make Word-to-World Connections

Person, Place, or Thing?

Directions: Follow these steps to complete the activity.

1. Read each word in the first column of the table below.

2. In the second column, write the name of a person, place, or thing that the word makes you think of.

3. In the third column, write a sentence or two explaining the connection. Try to use the key word in your explanation.

A sample response for *fictional* is completed for you.

This word...	...makes me think of...	Sentence
fictional	Narnia.	This is a *fictional* world that I read about in books by C. S. Lewis.
fictional		
theatrical		

continued

defiant		
dependent		
persistent		
angelic		
biographical		
appreciative		
competitive		
descriptive		

Master It : Use Words in Meaningful Ways

Pick One

Directions: In this activity, you'll write a *fictional, biographical,* or *descriptive* sketch. (A *sketch* is a short piece of writing that, in this case, captures a person, place, or thing.) Here's what to do:

1. **Pick one** type of sketch to write: fictional, biographical, or descriptive. For topic ideas, review your work in the Person, Place, or Thing? activity above.

2. **Research** information that you'll need to write your sketch. For instance, suppose you want to write a fictional sketch that takes place in Narnia. You should get one or more of the books in the Chronicles of Narnia series and review details of this fictional world.

3. **Write** a 200- to 300-word sketch of the person, place, or thing. In your writing, use at least two to five vocabulary words.

4. **Exchange** papers with a writing partner to get feedback. Read each other's sketches, and point out one strength and one weakness in the sketch. Help each other decide how to improve on the weakness.

5. **Write** the final copy of your sketch and submit it to your teacher.

List 8   Words with Adverb Suffixes

Study these three common adverb suffixes and some words (adverbs) that are formed with them. Read each word, what it means, and how it's used. Remember, an adverb describes a verb, adjective, or another adverb.

Suffix	Meaning	Examples
-ly	in a certain way	drama**tically**, histori**cally**, sole**ly**, triumphant**ly**, unanimous**ly**, visi**bly**
-ward	in the direction of	home**ward**, west**ward**
-wise	in the direction or way of	length**wise**, like**wise**

Word	What It Means	How It's Used
dramatically *(adv)* druh-MA-tih-klee	*in a* dramatic or striking *way*	The announcer paused *dramatically* before revealing the winner of the contest.
historically *(adv)* hi-STAWR-ih-klee	according to history	Do you think the author's description of ancient Greece is *historically* accurate?
solely *(adv)* SOHL-lee	not including anything else	He didn't like waiting tables; he did it *solely* for the good tips.
triumphantly *(adv)* try-UHM-fuhnt-lee	*in a* victorious *way*	The winner of the election walked *triumphantly* onto the stage.
unanimously *(adv)* yoo-NAN-uh-muhs-lee	with the agreement of all	All one hundred seventh graders voted *unanimously* to elect John as class president.
visibly *(adv)* VIZ-uh-bulee	*in a* visible *way*; so as can be seen	Daniela was *visibly* upset when she misplaced her MP3 player.
homeward *(adv)* HOHM-werd	toward home	After hours of hiking, we were at last heading *homeward*.

continued

westward *(adv)* WEST-werd	toward the west	The pioneers loaded up their wagons and traveled *westward*.
lengthwise *(adv)* LENGKTH-wahyz	*in the direction of* the length	Fold the paper *lengthwise* and label the two columns Pro and Con.
likewise *(adv)* LAHYK-wahyz	in the same manner; similarly	I nodded and smiled, and she did *likewise*.

Own It : Develop Your Word Understanding

Weekend Theater Review

Directions: In the following review of a play, vocabulary words are printed in bold type. Read the review. Then use your knowledge of the vocabulary words to answer the questions. After you complete the activity, explain some of your answers in a class discussion.

Weekend Theater Review	Questions
The seventh-grade production of **Homeward** Bound was a crowd-pleaser. The play is about a Confederate soldier's long walk home following the Civil War. As he trudges **westward**, the soldier speaks with numerous people. Each of them has passionate views on the war and its outcome. One of the delights of this play was its visual appeal. The costumes were **historically** accurate. **Likewise**, the sets were authentic to country roads in America in 1865. The main set was a dirt road running **lengthwise** across the stage. As the audience saw during the dust storm in Act 2, this road was made of real dirt!	1. Someone who is *homeward* bound is going _____. 2. You would look *westward* to see the sun _____ each day. 3. A *historically* accurate costume based on the 1860s would probably *not* have _____ on it. 4. A synonym of *likewise* is _____. 5. Would a road running *length-wise* across the stage run across the shortest or the longest part of the stage? _____. 6. In what way might an actor be *visibly* nervous?_____ _____

continued

Weekend Theater Review	Questions
Overall, the actors turned in fine performances. The star, Jackson Thomas, was **visibly** nervous in the first scene; however, he soon hit his stride. After the final scene, Jackson **triumphantly** returned to stage for a standing ovation.	**7.** When Jackson *triumphantly* returns for a standing ovation, he probably feels _____.

Link It: Make Word-to-World Connections

Movie Poster

Directions: In this activity, you will create a movie poster that shows your knowledge of the vocabulary words. To complete the activity, follow these steps:

1. Gather materials to create a movie poster about a movie you like. You'll need poster board, magazine cutouts, photocopies, your own artwork, paints, pens, or similar supplies.

2. Plan your poster. Besides planning images, think about how you can incorporate at least three of the vocabulary words. For example, you could make up one-line movie reviews, a statement telling about the plot, quotations from the actors, and so on.

3. Create the movie poster. Display your poster in class and point out the ways you used the vocabulary words to promote the movie.

Master It: Use Words in Meaningful Ways

Time Capsule

Directions: In this activity, you'll use the vocabulary words to create a time capsule. Here's what to do:

1. Use each vocabulary word to make a statement about your life, thoughts, goals, friends, and more. Focus on ideas relating to this calendar year or this school year. For instance, *historically*, what events does your school host each year (fall carnival, etc.)? What do you see when you look *westward* from the front door of your home? How will you *visibly* change in the future?

2. Collect a memento that corresponds to each statement. For instance, include a trinket from the fall carnival or a sketch of the view from your home. Write new sentences to go along with other mementos.

3. Use a shoe box, manila envelope, or other container as your time capsule. Fill it with your messages and mementos. Finally, seal the container and write a note on it stating when you will open it—say, five years from now. Your life now may be fascinating to your future self!

Wrapping Up: Review What You've Learned

Here's a brief summary of what you've studied in this chapter.

> A **suffix** is a group of letters added to the end of a base word or root so as to change its meaning or create a new word. Many words have more than one suffix.

> Every suffix has a particular meaning or meanings. Adding different suffixes to the same base word creates new words with different meanings.

> A suffix may have more than one meaning. Two different suffixes can have the same meaning.

> Adding a suffix can change a word from one part of speech to another.

> Some suffixes are spelled in more than one way.

> Suffixes help you identify a word's part of speech and see how the word relates to other words in the sentence.

> You've learned the following suffixes and words that contain them:

-age (condition of)

-cy (quality, condition, or fact of being)

-ity, -ty (quality, condition, or fact of being)

-ness (quality or condition of being)

-ate (to make)

-en (to make)

-fy (to make)

-ize (to make)

-al (of, suitable for, or relating to)

-ant, -ent (being or acting in a certain way)

-ic, -ical (like, relating to, or having the qualities of)

-ive (relating to or inclined to)

-ly (in a certain way)

-ward (in the direction of)

-wise (in the direction or way of)

Flaunt It: Show Your Word Understanding

In the following exercises, you'll demonstrate your understanding of each vocabulary word. You will use vocabulary words, or forms of the words, to complete sentences and to write sentences of your own.

A Sentence Completion

Directions: Circle the letter of the word that best completes each sentence.

1. Chris is so _____ that if he loses a board game, he angrily dumps the board and all the pieces on the floor.

   a. triumphant   **b.** appreciative
   c. competitive   **d.** angelic

2. If you have a bad cold, you can buy cough drops and medicine to help _____ some of the symptoms.

   a. beautify   **b.** alleviate
   c. clarify   **d.** simplify

3. In my opinion, _____ means standing by a friend even when that friend doesn't deserve it.

   a. secrecy   **b.** consciousness
   c. loyalty   **d.** likewise

4. This weekend, Sarah is going to help her aunt _____ her handwritten recipes. Then Sarah will e-mail copies to all the other cooks in the family.

   a. computerize   **b.** familiarize
   c. liberate   **d.** broaden

5. Your _____ impressed the Fitzgeralds so much that they would like you to babysit for them often.

   a. frequency   **b.** clumsiness
   c. accuracy   **d.** maturity

B Word Choice

Directions: Underline the word that best completes each sentence.

6. The (*shortage, persistence*) of rainfall has allowed a layer of dust and grime to settle upon the streets of the city.

7. My volleyball team was suffering from a lack of (*unity, defiance*), so we participated in a gym lock-in overnight to work on our team spirit.

8. The characters in *The Giver* seem so real to me that I have to remind myself that they are only (*biographical, fictional*).

9. Look (*visibly, westward*), and you will see the most beautiful sunset of the summer!

10. (*Historically, Theatrically*), Americans have valued their freedom and defended it fiercely.

 **Writing**

Directions: Follow the directions to write sentences using vocabulary words. Write your sentences on a separate sheet of paper.

11. Use *descriptive* to tell about a real person or a fictional character.

12. Use *homeward* to tell something about yourself.

13. Use *lengthwise* to give a friendly command.

14. Use *dependent* to tell something about a friend or family member.

15. Use *heighten* to tell about an emotion at a holiday.

16. Use *standardize* to tell what a baker might do when planning the sale of cookies.

17. Use *frequency* to ask a question to a friend.

18. Use *marriage* in a sentence that expresses an opinion.

19. Use *persistent* in a sentence that expresses a goal.

20. Use *shortage* in a statement about the supplies in a kitchen.

Activities à la Carte: Extend Your Word Knowledge

The activities on this page are presented à la carte, like items on a restaurant menu, meaning that you can choose from a variety of options. Your teacher may assign an activity or let you pick the one that tempts your appetite. If time allows, you might do more than one activity. All of the activities feature the same ingredient: **suffixes**. Dig in!

All My Friends Say . . .

If your friends could classify you as a suffix, what type would it be? Like noun suffixes, do you label everything and put everything in its place? Or are you bossy, telling people how to do something, like adverb suffixes? Get together with a few friends, and have fun classifying one another as noun, verb, adjective, or adverb suffixes. Then write a paragraph explaining how you were labeled, and why.

In Other Words

Do you speak a language other than English? Get out the sketch you wrote for the Pick One activity on page 41. Translate the sketch into a second language. What happens to the suffixes in words when you translate them? Do the translated words contain suffixes? Do the suffixes in the second language sound similar to the English versions? Share your translated sketch with someone who speaks the language.

Smart Aleck

Use suffixes to create your own slang words. Start by listing some words that you and your friends often use. Then play around with adding suffixes to morph (change) them into unique words that have meaning to you and your friends. Write a copy of your slang dictionary, available only to your closest friends.

In the News

Do you have access to a video recorder or a camera? Create a news story about suffixes in your community. Working with a partner, film short segments in which you stand before a store sign, poster, or other printed item and report on the presence (or absence) of suffixes. If you are using a camera, photograph the signs and use the photographs in a "live" broadcast to your class.

Can You Picture This?

Suffixes are like the tails of words. They are there at the end, not glamorous but useful. Use this idea to plan a short lesson on suffixes for younger students. Create visuals, such as a lion that has LOUD written on its body and LY written on its tail. What animal would help you teach *softness*? *Terrify*? Other suffixes? Get permission to teach your lesson to younger students at your school, library, or tutoring center.

Tell Me!

Find out what a dictionary can tell you about suffixes by looking up a few. If you use an online dictionary, type a hyphen before the suffix, as in *-ly*. Start by looking up a few suffixes taught in this lesson. Then look up some suffixes that weren't in this lesson, such as *-ous*, *-ment*, and *-able*. Enlighten your class with your findings.

Business or Pleasure?

What would you rather be reading instead of doing homework? Maybe a football playbook, love note, or graphic novel? Combine business with pleasure! Relax and read what you want to. Then jot down a list of words with suffixes appearing in what you read. Share the results with your class. Explain whether suffixes appeared rarely or frequently, and whether they were mostly one type (say, noun suffixes), or a mix of types.

Learning Words Through Roots

3

The next time you pass a tree, a bush, or a patch of grass, stop and stare. Notice that you can see some of the plant but not all of it. And the part that goes unseen? The roots! You know they're down there, but they remain unseen unless you dig them up.

In a similar way, the roots of words tend to remain unseen. They are not technically buried—they are right there in plain view. However, people don't often look for these word roots. It's as if they were buried.

Roots are a key building block of words. Combined with word parts such as prefixes and suffixes, roots form complete words. In this chapter, you'll practice "digging up" the roots of words so that you can study them. You'll learn some common roots, and you'll learn the meanings of words formed from these roots. Happy digging!

Objectives

In this chapter, you will learn

> What a root is

> Why you should know roots

> Words with Greek and Latin roots

Sneak Peek: Preview the Lesson

Agree or Disagree?

Read each statement at the top of the next page and decide whether you agree or disagree with it. If you agree, write YES on the line under Before Reading. If you disagree, write NO on that line.

After you complete the chapter, return to this page and fill out the After Reading column. Notice whether your new knowledge leads you to answer differently.

Before Reading   After Reading

_____ 1. A word can contain more than one root.   _____

_____ 2. Several roots can have the same meaning.   _____

_____ 3. A root can stand alone as a word.   _____

_____ 4. Roots of English words can come from
          other languages.   _____

_____ 5. A root appears only in the middle of a word.   _____

Ⓥocabulary Mini-Lesson: All About Roots

A **root** is the main word part that you can build different words on. As you read in Chapter 1, a root is different from a base word. A base word is a complete word and can stand alone. A root usually cannot stand alone as a word.

In Chapters 1 and 2, you saw examples of how roots are combined with prefixes and suffixes. What are the roots in the following words? What kind of word part is added to each root?

re-	+	*vers(e)* (turn)	=	reverse ("to turn back")
re-	+	*mit* (send)	=	remit ("to send back")
forti(s) (strong)	+	*-fy*	=	fortify ("to make strong")
satis (enough)	+	*-fy*	=	satisfy ("to make enough")

Why Learn This?

Like prefixes and suffixes, roots come from other languages, such as Greek and Latin. Knowing some common Greek and Latin roots will help you figure out the meanings of new words. In fact, some roots will help you understand a wide range of words in the same large "family." For example, the Latin root *scrib* or *script* comes from *scribere*, meaning "to write." The tree diagram on the next page shows you just *some* of the many words built on that root.

How does each word in this word family involve writing? Check a dictionary if you're not sure. Can you suggest any words to add?

Scrib, Script Word Family

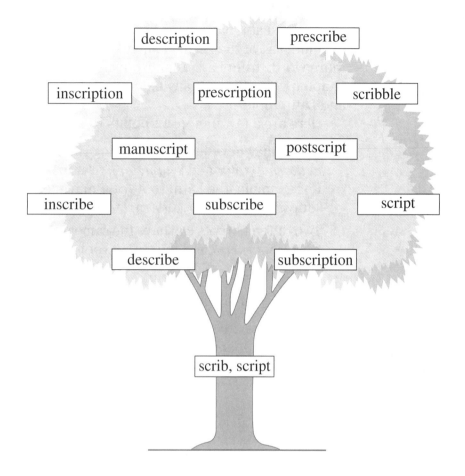

Prefixes, roots, and suffixes are often called the building blocks of words. By combining your knowledge of prefixes, roots, and suffixes, you'll be able to figure out many words by breaking them down into their parts. What parts make up the following words?

PREFIX	+	ROOT	+	SUFFIX	=	WORD
pre-	+	_dict_	+	_-able_	=	predictable
(before)		(say)		(able to be)		(able to be predicted)

The outcome of this chess match is not _predictable._

con-	+	_struct_	+	_-ive_	=	constructive
(together)		(build)		(inclined to)		(helpful)

Help your partner improve his writing skills by giving him _constructive_ criticism.

_ab-_	+	_rupt_	+	_-ly_	=	abruptly
(away from)		(break)		(in a certain way)		(suddenly)

The rope _abruptly_ snapped, and the boat drifted away.

Words to Know: Vocabulary Lists and Activities

Greek and Latin have contributed thousands of words that have become part of the English language. In fact, English contains more words from Latin than from any other language. In this chapter, you will see many examples of words built upon Greek and Latin roots.

Here are a few important points to remember.

> A root may have just one meaning (*meter* means "measure," as in *thermometer* and *kilometer*), or it may have more than one. For example, the Latin root *tract* may mean "pull," "move," or "draw," as in *tractor*, *subtract*, *attract*, and *distract*.

> Two different roots can have the same meaning. For instance, the Latin root *script* and the Greek root *graph* both mean "write":

> *script*: manuscript, inscription

> *graph*: autograph, paragraph

> Some roots are spelled in more than one way. For example, the root *pon* comes from Latin *ponere* and means "put" or "place" as in *postpone* and *opponent*. The same root is also spelled *pos*, as in *deposit* and *impose*.

List 9   Words with Greek Roots

Study the following list of Greek roots and words that are formed with them. Read each word, what it means, and how it's used.

Root	Meaning	Examples
aster, astr, astro	star	**aster**isk, **astro**nomy, dis**aster**
bio	life	**bio**graphy, **bio**logical
logy	the study of or science of	eco**logy**, theo**logy**
phon, phono	sound	**phon**etic, **phono**graph, sym**phon**y

Word	What It Means	How It's Used
asterisk (n) AS-tuh-risk	a star-shaped mark (*) that is used in printing or writing to indicate a footnote (literally, "little star")	The *asterisk* next to that word in the text directs the reader's attention to the note at the bottom of the page.

continued

astronomy *(n)* uh-STRON-uh-mee	the scientific study of the stars, planets, and other objects in the universe	People interested in *astronomy* use high-powered telescopes to look into space.
disaster *(n)* di-ZAS-ter	an event that causes great harm or damage (The "star" meaning relates to the idea that misfortune can be caused by the stars' influence. The prefix *dis-* is on List 1, page 5.)	The tornado was the worst *disaster* ever to affect our town.
biography *(n)* bie-OG-ruh-fee	a written account of a person's life	The author carefully researched Winston Churchill's life so that she could write a *biography* of the former British prime minister.
biological *(adj)* bie-uh-LOJ-i-kuhl	relating to biology, the scientific study of plant and animal life (The suffix *-ical* appears on List 7, page 38.)	The researcher hoped that her *biological* experiments would lead to a cure for the disease.
ecology *(n)* i-KOL-uh-jee	the scientific study of the relation between living things and their environment	Pollution is an important factor to consider when studying plant *ecology*.
theology *(n)* thee-AH-luh-jee	the study of religious faith	The university offers a course in *theology* that teaches about the various religions of the world.
phonetic *(adj)* fuh-NEH-tik	relating to or representing speech sounds	*Phonetic* spelling spells words the way they are pronounced.
phonograph *(n)* FOH-nuh-graf	an instrument for reproducing recorded sounds	Dad likes to play his favorite old records on a *phonograph*.
symphony *(n)* SIM-fuh-nee	a musical composition for an orchestra	Beethoven wrote many well-known *symphonies*.

Own It: Develop Your Word Understanding

You Be the Teacher

Directions: In this activity, you'll use scissors to cut the root out of a vocabulary word. Why? To teach your classmates a thing or two. Follow the steps at the top of the next page.

1. Your teacher will assign you a vocabulary word. Write your word in large block letters on a piece of paper. Set it aside.

2. Learn about your word. What does the word mean? What is the root? What is the root's meaning?

3. Grab a pair of scissors and the paper from step 1. It's showtime!

4. Stand in front of the class and hold up your word. Then do three things:

   a. Tell the class what the word means.

   b. Cut the root out of the word.

   c. Hold up the root and tell what it means.

Note: You may not be the first student to teach your word to the class. If your word seems familiar to students, that's great! That means everyone is learning the vocabulary words. Your lesson will reinforce their knowledge.

Link It: Make Word-to-World Connections

Have You Ever . . .

Directions: In this activity, you and your classmates will share personal experiences with the vocabulary words. Here's how the activity works:

1. Use a vocabulary word to write a question for your classmates. You may want to begin your question with the words *Have you ever . . .* or *Do you know. . . .* (Examples: Have you ever performed a *biological* experiment? Do you know what a *phonograph* looks like?)

2. One by one, students ask their questions to the class. In response, students raise hands to indicate an answer of *yes*. Your teacher will call on people to explain their answers. (Example answer: "I performed a *biological* experiment with ants by creating an ant farm in a glass jar.")

Master It: Use Words in Meaningful Ways

Did You Know?

Directions: In this activity, you will choose one vocabulary word to explore. Then you'll share a few facts about this word with your classmates. Follow the steps on the next page.

1. Review the list of vocabulary words and their meanings. Choose one word that seems interesting to you.

2. Find *two or three* facts about the word that you can share with your class. For instance, what's the difference between *astronomy* and astrology? What might you study in a class on *theology*? Useful sources of information include textbooks, encyclopedias, knowledgeable people, and articles.

3. Write a few sentences stating two or three facts about the vocabulary word. Here are some phrases you could use to begin the sentences:

   > Did you know that . . .

   > A surprising fact about (*vocabulary word*) is . . .

   > A question I had about (*vocabulary word*) was . . .

4. Practice reading your sentences aloud. Then read your sentences to your classmates.

List 10   Words with Latin Roots

You learned some Greek roots. Now study these Latin ones and ten words that are formed with them. Read each word, what it means, and how it's used.

Root	Meaning	Examples
ced, cede, ceed, cess	go or yield	ac**cess**, ex**ceed**
pend, pens	hang	ap**pend**ix, **pend**ing
spec, spect	see or look	**spec**ific, **spect**ator, **spec**ulate
vid, vis	see	e**vid**ent, super**vise**, **vis**ual

Word	What It Means	How It's Used
access *(n)* AK-ses	the right or ability to approach, enter, or use	Students have *access* to the school library every day.
exceed *(v)* ik-SEED	to go beyond	Drivers who *exceed* the speed limit will be stopped by the police.

continued

appendix *(n)* uh-PEN-diks	additional material at the end of a book or other written document	The *appendix* to our history textbook includes a list of political organizations.
pending *(adj)* PEN-ding	not yet decided	There are some *pending* issues we need to decide on before we can create our final product.
specific *(adj)* spi-SIF-ik	clearly expressed; precise; particular	Support your main idea with *specific* details.
spectator *(n)* SPEK-tay-ter	a person who sees or watches	*Spectators* lined the streets, watching the parade go by.
speculate *(v)* SPEK-yuh-layt	to think about the possibilities; ponder; consider	Scientists often *speculate* about the fate of the dinosaurs.
evident *(adj)* EV-i-duhnt	easy to see; clear; plain	It was *evident* from the applause that the audience enjoyed the show.
supervise *(v)* SOO-per-vize	to oversee or manage	Adults should *supervise* young children in the kitchen.
visual *(adj)* VIH-zhuh-wohl	related to seeing	The photographer became well known for her striking *visual* images.

Tip

The more word parts you learn, the more words you can add to your vocabulary and the better able you are to understand each word's meaning.

Get into the habit of looking at words carefully and thinking about their parts. For example, in Chapter 1, page 10, you learned the prefix *pre-*. In this chapter, you learned the root *cede*. How does your knowledge of these two parts make it easy to learn the word *precede*?

Own It: Develop Your Word Understanding

Draw It!

Directions: In this activity, you will draw simple sketches to help yourself remember the meaning of each vocabulary word. Follow these steps:

1. Study the list of vocabulary words and definitions.

2. Write a different vocabulary word in the upper corner of each box. (There are ten words and ten boxes.) Practice saying the word aloud.

3. Draw a simple picture that will help you remember the meaning of each word. For example, to remember *access*, you might draw a door labeled "Backstage Access." For *evident*, you might draw a face with a large nose on it with the caption "As evident as the nose on your face."

4. When you have finished filling in the chart, share your work with a classmate for further ideas and inspiration. Make any changes that you discover are needed.

My Memory Cues

Word: Sketch	Word: Sketch
Word: Sketch	Word: Sketch

continued

My Memory Cues

Word:
Sketch

Word:
Sketch

Word:
Sketch

Word:
Sketch

Word:
Sketch

Word:
Sketch

When I get my driver's license, I hope to have <u>access</u> to my mom's car. It's <u>evident</u> that I'm responsible, and I would never <u>exceed</u> the speed limit! But she said permission is still <u>pending</u>, based on whether or not I can keep up my grades until then.

Link It: Make Word-to-World Connections

Welcome to My World

Directions: In this activity, you'll work alone and then with a group to link vocabulary words to your world. Here's what to do:

1. Play around with the vocabulary words, using them to make statements about yourself, friends, family members, your neighborhood, or other aspects of your life. Write at least *five* sentences using vocabulary words (at least one word per sentence).

2. Choose *three* sentences that best describe your world. Cut your paper in strips, one sentence per strip.

3. In a small group, jumble everyone's sentences in a box. Take turns pulling out a sentence, reading it aloud, and guessing whose life it describes.

Master It: Use Words in Meaningful Ways

Your Turn to Teach

Directions: In this activity, you'll work in groups to teach a word to the rest of the class.

1. Your teacher will assign small groups, and give each group a different vocabulary word.

2. In your groups, decide how to teach your word's meaning to the class. You can use examples, draw on the board, etc.

3. Your teacher will call on groups to present to the class.

More About Words from Greek

If you look back at the word lists you've studied, you may notice an interesting difference between words that come from Greek and words that come from Latin. Words from Latin generally combine one root with a prefix, suffix, or both. Words from Greek, however, often (but not always) combine two roots. Compare these examples:

LATIN PREFIX + ROOT	LATIN ROOT + SUFFIX	GREEK ROOT + ROOT
avert	liberate	phonograph
inscribe	clarify	biology
precede	dependent	astrology

Greek roots are also interesting in that so many of the nouns can be changed to adjectives by adding the suffix *-ic* or *-ical* (see List 7, page 38) and to adverbs by adding the suffix -*ly* (see List 8, page 42). Look at these examples:

NOUN	ADJECTIVE	ADVERB
(Greek root)	(adds -*ic* or –*ical*)	(adds -*ly*)
astronomy	astronomic or astronomical	astronomically
biography	biographic or biographical	biographically
ecology	ecologic or ecological	ecologically
etymology	etymological	etymologically
symphony	symphonic	symphonically

Wrapping Up: Review What You've Learned

Here's a brief summary of what you've studied in this chapter.

> A **root** is a word part from which other words are formed. A root differs from a base word. A base word can stand alone, while a root usually cannot.

> Like prefixes and suffixes, roots also come from other languages, such as Greek and Latin.

> A root may have just one meaning, or it may have more than one.

> Two different roots can have the same meaning.

> Some roots are spelled in more than one way.

> While a root by itself may not look familiar, knowing its meaning will give you an important clue to the meaning of every word built on that root. Some roots will help you understand large "families" of words.

> You've learned the following roots and words that contain them:

aster, astr, astro (**star**)

bio (**life**)

logy (**the study or science of**)

phon, phono (**sound**)

ced, cede, ceed, cess (**go or yield**)

pend, pens (**hang**)

spec, spect (**see or look**)

vid, vis (**see**)

Flaunt It: Show Your Word Understanding

In the following exercises, you'll demonstrate your understanding of each vocabulary word. You will use vocabulary words, or forms of the words, to complete sentences and to write sentences of your own.

 A **Matching**

Directions: Match the underlined word to its definition. Write the letter of the definition on the line provided.

_____ **1.** I found a site on the Internet where I was able to listen to a beautiful <u>symphony</u> written by Franz Schubert, an Austrian musician.

_____ **2.** At the high school football game, <u>spectators</u> ate hot dogs and cheered for their team.

_____ **3.** In <u>biological</u> warfare, germs are used as weapons of attack.

_____ **4.** Please give me a <u>specific</u> reason why you don't like my plan.

_____ **5.** In a <u>biography</u> of Jane Goodall, I learned how she became world-famous for her study of chimpanzees.

_____ **6.** I typed an <u>asterisk</u> next to the word *free*; then, at the bottom of the page, I typed, "While supplies last."

_____ **7.** A <u>phonetic</u> spelling of the word *knight* would not include the letter *k*, since this letter is not pronounced in the word.

_____ **8.** There is some <u>pending</u> business that I must deal with before I can make a final decision.

_____ **9.** Sometimes I <u>speculate</u> about life on other planets. Do you?

_____ **10.** For <u>access</u> to the hiking trail, follow the signs to the trailhead.

a. to think about the possibilities; ponder; consider

b. a written account of a person's life

c. the right or ability to approach, enter, or use

d. a star-shaped mark (*) that is used in printing or writing to indicate a footnote

e. relating to or representing speech sounds

f. people who see or watch

g. a musical composition for an orchestra

h. not decided; awaiting a decision or action

i. relating to biology; the scientific study of plant and animal life

j. clearly expressed; precise; particular

 **Sentence Completion**

Directions: Circle the letter of the word that best completes each sentence.

11. When we studied _____ in science class, I was especially interested in the details about how tornadoes form.

a. astronomy **b.** disasters
c. biographies **d.** asterisks

12. Dad has a collection of old vinyl records, but he doesn't have a/an _____ to use for playing them.

a. phonograph **b.** symphony
c. phonetic **d.** ecology

13. Visitors to the candy factory may take two free samples from the display. Please do not _____ the limit.

a. access **b.** access
c. speculate **d.** exceed

14. You will find a list of useful Web sites in the book's _____.

a. appendix **b.** theology
c. evidence **d.** spectators

15. When I read textbooks, I learn the most from chapters that have _____ images, such as tables and photographs, that help explain complex information.

a. specifics **b.** supervise
c. visual **d.** biological

C **Writing**

Directions: Write one or more sentences to answer each question. Be sure to use the vocabulary word, and write your sentences on a separate sheet of paper.

16. What has a friend done to *exceed* your patience?

17. What is one fact that is *evident* about your personality?

18. Would you rather *supervise* children or dogs for an afternoon?

19. Which planet (besides Earth) would you most want to study for an *astronomy* project?

20. What was the last *disaster* that happened to you?

Activities à la Carte: Extend Your Word Knowledge

The activities on this page are presented à la carte, like items on a restaurant menu, meaning that you can choose from a variety of options. Your teacher may assign an activity or let you pick the one that tempts your appetite. If time allows, you might do more than one activity. All of the activities feature the same ingredient: **roots**. Dig in!

Family Reunion

Choose a Greek or Latin root and create a poster showing a family of words that use this root. On the poster, include a definition of the root's meaning and list as many words as you can discover that use this root. Colorful paints or artwork will make the poster eye-catching. Display your creation in class.

Just a Little Thing

A book's appendix is one thing, but the human body's appendix is something else entirely. Find out about the human appendix and report back to your class. Answer questions such as What is it? What does it look like? Why is it there? and What is appendicitis?

Root Canal

Have you ever had a *root* canal? Have you eaten a *root* vegetable? Have you traced your family's *roots*? These are just a few of the many uses of *root*, a multiple-meaning word. Make a poster or computer presentation to teach your classmates different uses of *root*. Be sure to use visuals, along with words, to get your ideas across.

Tinker with It

Tinker with the vocabulary words in this chapter, changing them into other parts of speech. You'll notice that the same root is evident in each word form. For instance, *visual* becomes *visualize* and *visually*. Share some of the results with your class. Discuss how this knowledge of roots and word forms could come in handy.

Movie Pitch

Use vocabulary words in this chapter to inspire ideas for a movie. Alone or with a partner, write a plot summary to tell what your movie is about. Write a list of characters with brief descriptions of each. Finally, pitch your movie idea to the class. Ask for a show of hands indicating who would go see your movie.

 ## Compare and Contrast

Find out if a word with a Greek or Latin root in English has the same root if translated into another language. But don't stop there—translate the word into three different languages. You can use an online translation tool (www.translation.langenberg.com is good), or use translation dictionaries in a library. Create a table showing the results and draw some conclusions from these results. Share your findings with others who enjoy languages and translation.

Tongue Twisters

Use vocabulary words to write tongue twisters. The key to tricky twisters is to use *alliteration,* or the same sound at the beginnings of words close together. For instance, *Specific spectators speculate about the suspension of the supervisor* is a tongue twister using words from List 10. Create a few twisters and hold a contest to see who can say them fastest without making a mistake.

When I Grow Up

Get some friends together and have fun with vocabulary words. Create a book called *When I Grow Up.* Devote each page of the book to a different vocabulary word and relate the word to a profession or activity. For instance, on one page you could write, "When I grow up, I want to *exceed* the speed limit." Illustrate the sentence with a drawing (or photo) of a racetrack. Get the idea? Go for it!

Forming Words with Prefixes and Suffixes

4

F or a food lover, it is fun to experiment with ingredients, adding new twists to old recipes and inventing new dishes. You may have done this yourself. *What would happen if I added cinnamon to the chili?* or *I like the pancake recipe, but I want to add mashed banana to it.* By studying recipes and experimenting with ingredients, you gain confidence and skill as a cook.

In the same way, you can have fun studying and playing with words. You can study "recipes" such as rules for adding prefixes and suffixes to roots. You can play around with combining various word parts to build your vocabulary. When you see a new or fascinating word, you can look it up in the ultimate word cookbook, a dictionary. You'll do all these things in this chapter. Along the way, you'll gain confidence and skill as a reader and writer.

Objectives

In this chapter, you will learn

> How to add prefixes and suffixes to form new words

> Common words with multiple word parts (prefixes *and* suffixes)

Sneak Peek: Preview the Lesson

Skim and Scan

As you may know, you can determine what a chapter is about by skimming and scanning it. To **skim** a chapter, you run your eyes over the headings, tables, and other features to get an idea of what the chapter is about. To **scan** a chapter, you run your eyes over headings and paragraphs, looking for particular words or ideas. Skimming and scanning are helpful because they allow you to get useful information quickly.

1. What can you find out by skimming this chapter? **Skim** the headings, tables, and any other features that stand out to you. Then write a few phrases or sentences identifying what topics you think the chapter will cover.

_____

_____

_____

2. **Scan** the chapter for key words such as _prefix, suffix, root,_ and _base._ Based on your scan, what do you expect the chapter to teach you?

_____

_____

_____

Vocabulary Mini-Lesson: How to Add Prefixes and Suffixes

It's usually easy to add a prefix to a word. Just keep all the letters of both the prefix and the base word and put them together.

Study the examples below, which use some of the prefixes you learned in Chapter 1. Notice that no letters are left out or changed. Even when the last letter of the prefix is the same as the first letter of the base word, keep both letters. For example, adding _dis-_ to _satisfied_ gives you _di<u>ss</u>atisfied._

PREFIX	+	BASE WORD	=	NEW WORD
dis	+	satisfied	=	dissatisfied
non	+	fiction	=	nonfiction
pre	+	view	=	preview
mono	+	rail	=	monorail
fore	+	tell	=	foretell
over	+	load	=	overload

Do you see that no letters are changed or dropped?

Now that you've seen how to add prefixes, let's look at how to add suffixes. Most of the time, you'll keep all the letters of both the suffix and the word and not drop, change, or add any letters. Look at the following examples.

BASE WORD	+	SUFFIX	=	NEW WORD
leak	+	-age		leakage
bankrupt	+	-cy		bankruptcy
frail	+	-ty		frailty

stubborn	+	-ness	stubbornness
sharp	+	-en	sharpen
legal	+	-ize	legalize
rent	+	-al	rental
absorb	+	-ent	absorbent
hero	+	-ic	heroic
attract	+	-ive	attractive
appropriate	+	-ly	appropriately

In forming these words, there are no letters changed or omitted.

However, sometimes adding a suffix *does* affect the spelling of a word. This usually happens when you add suffixes to words ending in *y* or silent *e*. Let's look at both of these cases, using suffixes that you learned in Chapter 2.

Adding Suffixes to Words That End in *Y*

When it comes to attaching suffixes, words ending in *y* can cause some confusion. That's because not all *y*-ending words follow the same rule. The key is to look at the letter *before* the *y*.

> If the letter before the *y* is a *consonant*, change the *y* to *i* before adding the suffix.

BASE WORD	+	SUFFIX	=	NEW WORD
marry	+	-age	=	marriage
hasty	+	-ness	=	hastiness
beauty	+	-fy	=	beautify
fantasy	+	-ize	=	fantasize
defy	+	-ant	=	defiant
angry	+	-ly	=	angrily

Note: There are a few exceptions to this rule, such as *shyness*, *shyly*, *dryness*, *slyly*, and *wryly*.

> If the letter before the *y* is a *vowel*, do *not* change the *y* to *i* before adding the suffix.

BASE WORD	+	SUFFIX	=	NEW WORD
gray	+	-ness	=	grayness
betray	+	-al	=	betrayal
coy	+	-ly	=	coyly
buy	+	-er	=	buyer
key	+	-less	=	keyless

Note: One exception to this rule is *daily*.

Adding Suffixes to Words That End with a Silent *E*

Many words end in a silent *e*. This means that the *e* is not pronounced, as in *alive* and *blame*. There are two general rules for attaching suffixes to words ending with a silent *e*. The key is to look at the first letter of the suffix.

> If the suffix starts with a *vowel*, drop the silent *e*.

BASE WORD	+	SUFFIX	=	NEW WORD
store	+	-age	=	storage
sincere	+	-ity	=	sincerity
immune	+	-ize	=	immunize
nature	+	-al	=	natural

Note: There are some exceptions to this rule. Words ending in *ge*, such as *courageous* and *outrageous*, keep the silent *e*. In addition, words ending in *able* sometimes keep the silent *e*. Examples: *agreeable, knowledgeable, changeable, manageable, noticeable,* and *rechargeable*. Other *able* words do follow the rule and drop the silent *e*: *believable, desirable, usable, lovable, excusable*.

> If the suffix starts with a *consonant*, keep the silent *e*.

BASE WORD	+	SUFFIX	=	NEW WORD
safe	+	-ty	=	safety
false	+	-ness	=	falseness
home	+	-ward	=	homeward
like	+	-wise	=	likewise
tame	+	-ly	=	tamely
encourage	+	-ment	=	encouragement
disgrace	+	-ful	=	disgraceful

Note: Exceptions to this rule include: *judgment, argument,* and *truly*.

> However, when you change an adjective ending in *-le* to an adverb ending in *-ly*, you drop the silent *e*:

ADJECTIVE	+	SUFFIX	=	ADVERB
horrible	+	-ly	=	horribly
possible	+	-ly	=	possibly
legible	+	-ly	=	legibly
incredible	+	-ly	=	incredibly

Words to Know: Vocabulary Lists and Activities

Many words contain two or more prefixes or suffixes. Your knowledge of word parts can help you figure out the meaning of such words. Study the following lists. The letters in dark type are prefixes and suffixes that you learned in Chapters 1 and 2. You may recognize some other word parts as well.

List 11   Words with Multiple Parts

Read each word, what it means, and how it's used.

Word	What It Means	How It's Used
abrupt**ness** *(n)* uh-BRUHPT-ness	suddenness; unexpectedness	The *abruptness* with which Mr. Dixon left the room made us wonder if he was feeling ill.
absorb**ent** *(adj)* ab-SAWR-buhnt	able to absorb or soak up	This sponge is *absorbent* enough to wipe up all the spilled water from the counter.
attract**iveness** *(n)* uh-TRAK-tiv-ness	the quality of being attractive; pleasant appearance	The model's carefully applied makeup adds to her *attractiveness*.
conspiracy *(n)* kuhn-SPIR-uh-see	a secret joining together in order to plan and carry out an unlawful or harmful act; plot	Military officials were involved in a *conspiracy* to take over the government.
conveni**ent** *(adj)* kuhn-VEEN-yuhnt	easy to do or use; suitable	Our savings bank has many *convenient* locations.
descript**ively** *(adv)* di-SKRIP-tiv-lee	in a way that describes	The author writes so *descriptively* that readers can clearly picture the scene.
disability *(n)* dis-uh-BIHL-ih-tee	a condition that may reduce or interfere with certain physical or mental activities	The injured soldier worked hard to overcome his *disability*.
discontent**edly** *(adv)* dis-kuhn-TEN-tid-lee	in a way that shows displeasure or unhappiness	The students grumbled *discontentedly* when the teacher announced there would be a test the following day.

continued

| dishonestly *(adv)*
dis-ON-ist-lee | in a way that is not truthful | "Did you earn this money," Freya asked, "or did you get it *dishonestly*?" |
| excessively *(adv)*
ik-SES-iv-lee | beyond what would be expected; extremely (*Note:* You studied the root *cess* in Chapter 3, page 57.) | Police suspect the man is hiding something because he seems *excessively* nervous. |

Own It: Develop Your Word Understanding

Exploring Key Words

Directions: Work with a partner to complete the activity. Each of you should complete five of the graphic organizers. Then share your results. For each graphic organizer, follow these steps:

1. Study the vocabulary word and its definition in the list above. Then use your own words and ideas to write a definition in the center box, below.

2. Play around with the word's parts—adding and subtracting them—to create other forms of the word. (For instance, *dishonest* is an adjective form of the adverb *dishonestly*.) Write these words in the first box.

3. In the third box, sketch or write a clue to help you remember the key word's meaning.

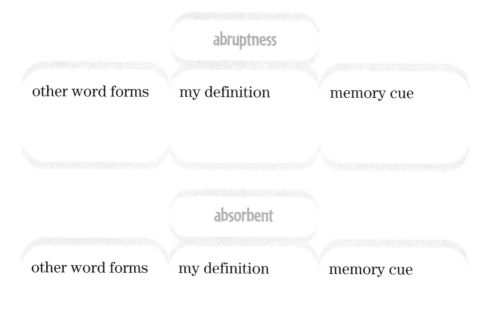

abruptness

other word forms   my definition   memory cue

absorbent

other word forms   my definition   memory cue

attractiveness

other word forms   my definition   memory cue

conspiracy

other word forms   my definition   memory cue

convenient

other word forms   my definition   memory cue

descriptively

other word forms   my definition   memory cue

disability

other word forms   my definition   memory cue

discontentedly

other word forms   my definition   memory cue

dishonestly

other word forms   my definition   memory cue

excessively

other word forms   my definition   memory cue

Link It: Make Word-to-World Connections

Me, Myself, and I

Directions: Follow these steps to complete the activity. Your teacher may ask you to work with a partner.

1. Think about how the key word—or another form of the word—relates to you. For instance, can you use the word in a description of yourself? In a comment about a friend? In a description of a dream or favorite activity? In a statement about your community?

2. In the space beside each key word, write a sentence or two telling what the word has to do with you and your world. Be sure to use the key word in your response!

Key Word	What Does This Word Have to Do with Me?
abruptness	
absorbent	
attractiveness	
conspiracy	
convenient	
descriptively	
disability	
discontentedly	
dishonestly	
excessively	

Master It: Use Words in Meaningful Ways

Word Problems

Directions: In a class or small group discussion, answer each of the following questions. Explain your reasoning.

1. How might a *disability* affect a person's life *excessively*?
2. Is *attractiveness* always *convenient*?
3. How could an *absorbent* product be marketed *dishonestly*?
4. Do people usually respond *discontentedly* to news of a *conspiracy*?
5. Is it possible to write *descriptively* with *abruptness*?

List 12   Words with Multiple Parts

Here are some additional words that are made of more than one part. Read each word, what it means, and how it's used.

Word	What It Means	How It's Used
disunity *(n)* dis-YOO-ni-tee	the condition of not being united; disagreement	Political leaders tried to resolve the *disunity* among ethnic groups.
geographically *(adv)* jee-uh-GRAF-i-kuhl-lee	with regard to geography	England and France are *geographically* separated by the English Channel.
inclusive *(adj)* in-KLOO-siv	including everything; complete	The treasurer prepared an *inclusive* budget, listing all the expected expenses for the coming year.
independently *(adv)* in-di-PEN-duhnt-lee	on one's own; separately from others (*Note*: You studied the root *pend* in Chapter 3, page 57.)	Some students like to team up with a partner, while others prefer to work *independently*.
insistent *(adj)* in-SIS-tuhnt	demanding attention; impossible to ignore	I buried my head under the pillow, but the *insistent* ringing of the telephone forced me to get up.
microscopic *(adj)* mie-kruh-SKAH-pik	requiring a microscope to be seen; tiny	Medical researchers examined *microscopic* cells, searching for clues to the disease.
monopolize *(v)* muh-NAH-puh-lize	to take control of; dominate	Anna talked so much that she *monopolized* the conversation.
predictive *(adj)* pri-DIK-tiv	likely to predict or forsee	Are good grades in high school *predictive* of success on the job?
unify *(v)* YOO-nuh-fie	to combine into one; bring together; unite	Voters hoped that a strong leader would *unify* the nation.
universal *(adj)* yoo-nuh-VUR-suhl	included or occurring everywhere	Love is a *universal* emotion.

Own It: Develop Your Word Understanding

Break It Up!

Directions: Your teacher will divide the class into ten small groups. Each group will be assigned one vocabulary word. In your group, follow these steps:

1. Break the word up into its parts. You'll have a root or base word plus one or more prefixes and suffixes. Write each word part on an index card.

2. On the backs of the cards, write definitions for the word parts. For instance, you know that *-fy* is a verb suffix meaning "to make" (see List 6, page 34). And a dictionary will tell you that the root of *unify* is *uni*, meaning "one" (read the etymology part of the word's entry).

3. Read your vocabulary word aloud to the class. Then identify the word parts and tell how they work together to form the key word.

Our lunch group is very inclusive—we don't care who sits with us; we're friendly to everyone. One thing we don't like is when someone tries to monopolize the conversation, though. It's better when everyone gets a chance to sound off.

Link It: Make Word-to-World Connections

Have You Ever . . .

Directions: Your teacher will get the activity started by asking a student one of the questions in the box on the next page. That person answers by saying yes or no and giving an explanation. Then that person asks someone else a question.

You can use one of the questions in the box or make up your own question using a vocabulary word.

Have you ever . . .

. . . visited *geographically* similar places (towns, states, countries)?

. . . paid an *inclusive* fee (such as for camp, an art class, etc.)?

. . . completed a project *independently*, start to finish?

. . . been *insistent*?

. . . felt fearful of or disgusted by *microscopic* germs?

. . . *monopolized* someone's time?

. . . wondered if your parents' looks are *predictive* of yours at that age?

. . . tried to *unify* people around a cause?

. . . felt *disunity* among people in a school or community?

. . . thought that people should have *universal* rights?

Master It: Use Words in Meaningful Ways

If You Wrote the News

Directions: Imagine that you are a television news reporter. Your assignment? Attract young viewers by reporting on a high-interest topic. Work with a partner, if your teacher approves, and follow these steps:

1. Study the list of vocabulary words. Think about how some of them relate to a topic of interest to you. (Topic ideas: current events, music, sports, books, movies, lifestyle/human interest.)

2. Write a 200-word news report on your chosen topic. Use as many vocabulary words (or forms of the words) as possible.

3. Prepare visuals for your report. These may include magazine cutouts, sketches, charts, or similar pieces relating to your news story.

4. Present your report live to the class. *Alternative:* If you have access to the necessary equipment, record your news segment and play it for the class.

Wrapping Up: Review What You've Learned

Here's a brief summary of what you've studied in this chapter.

> In general, to add a prefix to a base word, keep all the letters of both the prefix and the word, even when the last letter of the prefix is the same as the first letter of the word.

> Attaching a suffix to a word is a little trickier than adding a prefix. Most of the time, you keep all the letters of both the suffix and the word and not drop, change, or add any letters. However, sometimes special rules apply.

> To add a suffix to a word that ends in y, look at the letter before the y. If the letter before the y is a consonant, change the y to i before adding the suffix. If the letter before the y is a vowel, do *not* change the y to i before adding the suffix.

> To add a suffix to a word that ends in a silent e, look at the first letter of the suffix. If the suffix starts with a vowel, drop the silent e before adding the suffix. If the suffix starts with a consonant, keep the silent e. (But: When changing an adjective ending in -*le* to an adverb ending in -*ly*, drop the silent e.)

Chapter Review Exercises

Flaunt It: Show Your Word Understanding

In the following exercises, you'll demonstrate your understanding of each vocabulary word. You will use vocabulary words, or forms of the words, to complete sentences and to write sentences of your own.

A Word Bank

Directions: Choose a word from the box to complete each sentence. Write the word on the line provided. Each word may be used only once.

> absorbent   insistent   microscopic   conspiracy   geographically
> convenient   predictive   excessively   disability   independently

1. Mike is doing his science project on cells, which are _____ building blocks of the human body.

2. Sometimes Naomi feels too rushed to eat breakfast, but her mother is always _____ that she eat something, even if it's only dry toast.

3. Your sprained ankle is only a short-term _____. You'll be playing basketball again in no time!

4. This glossy magazine page is not very _____; on the other hand, this newspaper easily soaks up water.

5. Mr. Golde said, "You may work _____ to complete the assignment, or you may choose to work with a partner."

6. Tiger Woods's interest in golf as a child was _____ of his love of the sport as an adult.

7. Janna uses her cell phone _____; as a result, she has a huge phone bill each month.

8. The police have uncovered a/an _____ to steal concert tickets and sell them illegally.

9. Since you live near me, it would be _____ for us to carpool to school.

10. Carlos and I are _____ separated by a great distance, but we are emotionally close because we exchange e-mails nearly every day.

B   Sentence Completion

Directions: Circle the letter of the word that best completes each sentence.

11. The _____ of your voice suggests that you are angry with me.

    a. conspiracy   **b.** attractiveness
    c. convenience   **d.** abruptness

12. When the athletes were told to run four more laps around the track, they grumbled _____.

    a. discontentedly   **b.** dishonestly
    c. geographically   **d.** microscopically

13. Your fee for the field trip is _____ of entry to the exhibit, lunch, and one souvenir.

    a. descriptive   **b.** inclusive
    c. excessive   **d.** predictive

14. The desire for close relationships is a _____ need.

    a. microscopic   **b.** inclusive
    c. unity   **d.** universal

15. As captain, I have made it my goal to _____ this team, inspire this team, and lead this team to victory!

    a. monopolize   **b.** disable
    c. unify   **d.** insist

C   Writing

Directions: Follow the directions to write sentences using vocabulary words. Write your sentences on a separate sheet of paper.

16. Use *attractiveness* in a declarative sentence (sentence that makes a statement).

17. Use *descriptively* in an imperative sentence (sentence that makes a command).

18. Use *dishonestly* in an interrogative sentence (sentence that asks a question).

19. Use *disunity* in an exclamatory sentence (sentence that expresses strong emotion).

20. Use *monopolize* in a declarative sentence.

Activities à la Carte: Extend Your Word Knowledge

The activities on this page are presented à la carte, like items on a restaurant menu, meaning that you can choose from a variety of options. Your teacher may assign an activity or let you pick the one that tempts your appetite. If time allows, you might do more than one activity. All of the activities feature the same ingredient: **word parts**. Dig in!

Disc Jockey

If you love music *and* love to talk, you may be a DJ at heart. To give this enterprise a whirl, host a party where you'll be the DJ. Plan the music to fit the party's theme, mood, or purpose. Then write snippets of chatter to read between song sets. Use some of the vocabulary words to inspire topics and ideas. Finally, party, party, party!

You Crack Me Up

Dust off your funny bone and grab a pencil. Create a single-frame cartoon using a vocabulary word (or form of a word) from this chapter. For instance, how would you illustrate the quip "Myrtle was *geographically* challenged"? or "*Conveniently*, Horace had a pocketful of marshmallows"?

What's a Newbery?

Learn about the Newbery Medal at www.ala.org, the Web site of the American Library Association. Then study the titles of winning books. What prefixes and suffixes do you recognize? What roots and base words are familiar to you? Are titles of winning books typically formed of multipart words or simpler words? Share your findings with your class and recommend a few books that sound interesting.

Spare Change

Earn money by marketing your services as a babysitter, dog walker, yard cleaner, or all-purpose helper. Using new words you've learned, create a flyer. On it, hook clients with a rhetorical question such as, "Does housecleaning *monopolize* all your free time?" or "Do your dogs beg *discontentedly* for frequent walks?"

Then sell your service: "Hire me to bring *microscopic* cleanliness to your home." Finally, state your pay rate and contact information.

The Write Stuff

Compete with friends to see who can use word parts in this chapter to create the most new words in five minutes. Open your book to the two word lists (pages 71 and 76). Then set a timer for five minutes. Create new words and word forms by taking roots and adding different prefixes and suffixes. Then give your new words a reality check—are they real words? Ask your teacher if you can post your list on a class bulletin board.

¡Que Misterioso!

Translate each word in this chapter's word lists into a second language. Is there a direct translation for each word, or must you use a phrase? Can you break the translated word into the same parts as those in the English word? Would you say that one language relies on prefixes and suffixes more than the other language, or do they use these word parts about equally? Share your findings with someone who's interested in languages.

Fool Me Once

Use word parts from Chapters 1–4 of this book to create real-sounding **fake** words. A few examples to get you started are *attractivity, presorbent,* and *unicy.* Write a real or a fake word on index cards. Test friends and friendly adults to see who can sort real from fake.

Learning Words from Other Sources

5

Objectives

In this chapter, you will learn

> How new words come into our language from foreign languages, from mythology, and from the names of people, places, or things

> Common words from some of these various sources

I f you have a brother or sister, then you have probably experienced "copycat syndrome": a sibling wears your clothes, imitates your body language, or echoes your words. You yourself may have borrowed a sibling's or classmate's personal style or slang words. In fact, it's rare for a person *not* to borrow from others.

Languages are like siblings. They borrow from one another, sometimes adding their own twist to the borrowed word and sometimes using the word without changes. The English language is no exception. Some English words are borrowed from other languages. Some are based on gods and goddesses in ancient myths. Some come from the names of people and places. In this chapter, you'll learn a wide range of words from several different sources.

Sneak Peek: Preview the Lesson

Beg, Borrow, or Steal

The following table lists a few sources of English words in the first column. To become familiar with each type of source, respond to the questions in the second column. *Hint:* You may need to consult a reference source for help with unfamiliar terms.

Some Sources of Words	Questions for Thought
foreign languages	What are the names of some foreign languages? Do you ever use a word from one of these languages when you're speaking English? Explain.
mythology	What are myths? Can you name any characters from myths?
proper nouns	What are proper nouns? Can you think of any words formed from proper nouns?

Vocabulary Mini-Lesson: Words Come from Foreign Languages

What do you think the following words have in common?

adobe	macho	taco
fiesta	rodeo	tornado

If you guessed that all of these words have been adopted into English from Spanish, you're correct! In fact, many familiar words come not only from Spanish but from languages around the world.

Words from foreign languages have been added to English over hundreds of years, and they are still being added today. Over the centuries, whenever English speakers came into contact with people from other cultures through trade, travel, or war, they adopted or "borrowed" some of their words. These words may not seem foreign to us, either because their form and spelling have changed or simply because we are so used to hearing them. Did you know, for example, that *yogurt* is a Turkish word, while *kindergarten* comes from German (*kinder*, "children" + *garten*, "garden")? You may be surprised at the origin of some of the words in the following lists.

ords to Know: Vocabulary Lists and Activities

In this section, you'll study two lists of words from a wide variety of languages, including Arabic, Italian, and Russian.

List 13   Words from Foreign Languages

Here are common words from five different foreign languages. Read each word, its source, what it means, and how it's used.

Word	Its Source	What It Means	How It's Used
algebra *(n)* AL-juh-bruh	Arabic	a branch of mathematics	In *algebra*, letters are used to represent numbers, as in $x + y = 10$.
boomerang *(n)* BOO-muh-rang	Australian	a flat, curved piece of wood, used as a weapon, that can be thrown so that it will return to the thrower	The *boomerang* flew in a wide arc and came back to me.
brigade *(n)* bri-GAYD	Italian	a large military unit	All the soldiers in the *brigade* had great respect for the general.
cavalry *(n)* KAV-uhl-ree	Italian	originally, a military unit that fought on horseback, but now may use motorized vehicles	The outnumbered troops were relieved when the *cavalry* came to their aid.
confetti *(n)* kuhn-FEHT-tee	Italian	small pieces of colored paper made for throwing at celebrations	People tossed *confetti* from their windows as the parade passed.
croissant *(n)* kruh-SAHNT	French	a flaky roll shaped like a crescent	Nicole ate a *croissant* for breakfast.
czar *(n)* zahr	Russian	formerly, an emperor of Russia	Alexander I was the Russian *czar* from 1801 to 1825.
debris *(n)* duh-BREE	French	the remains of something that has been broken or destroyed	*Debris* from the shipwreck washed up on shore.
debut *(n)* day-BYOO	French	first public appearance	The young woman made her acting *debut* in a horror film.
etiquette *(n)* ET-i-ket	French	the behavior and manners considered acceptable or required in social situations	Proper *etiquette* requires diners to eat their soup without slurping.

Own It: Develop Your Word Understanding

Sensory Appeal

Directions: Study the list of vocabulary words and their meanings. Then take a moment to let each word come alive in your imagination. How? Think about how each word might appeal to one of the five senses. For instance, *debut* may appeal to your sense of hearing as you imagine an actor making his debut in musical theater.

Write each vocabulary word and a brief description of its appeal to you in one of the boxes that follow. You may record a word in more than one box.

Sense	How Each Vocabulary Word Appeals to That Sense
sight	
hearing	

continued

taste

touch

smell

During the pep rally last Friday, the soccer team got to <u>debut</u> their new uniforms. People cheered and threw black-and-orange <u>confetti</u> (our school colors). The gym was a mess afterwards, though—there was lots of <u>debris</u> covering the floor!

Link It: Make Word-to-World Connections

Where in the World?

Directions: Where in *your* world would you most likely encounter the things named by the vocabulary words? With a partner, discuss how you might encounter these people, things, and ideas. Then write each word in one of the boxes on the next page. *Bonus:* Add your own heading to the empty box and add words to this box too. (You may write a word in more than one box.)

In a class discussion, explain your categorization of the words.

at home   **in a class**

out having fun

Master It: Use Words in Meaningful Ways

Pick Three

Directions: In this activity, you'll help classmates become familiar with three vocabulary words that you know something about. Follow these steps:

1. Pick three vocabulary words that are familiar or interesting to you. (For ideas, review the two activities previous to this one.)

2. Write two or three sentences about each of the three words. Do your best to make the meaning of the word clear in the context of what you write. For instance, you could give specific examples of table *etiquette* or describe what a *boomerang* looks like and how to throw it.

3. Your teacher will pronounce each vocabulary word aloud. After saying each word, he or she will ask students to read sentences that tell about that word.

List 14   Words from Foreign Languages

Learn these additional words from various foreign languages. Read each word, what it means, and how it's used.

Word	Its Source	What It Means	How It's Used
fiancé (male), **fiancée** (female) *(n)* fee-ahn-SAY	French	a man or woman engaged to be married	After Elena accepted my marriage proposal, my *fiancée* and I celebrated at a fancy restaurant.
influenza *(n)* in-floo-EN-zuh	Italian	a contagious disease caused by a virus	The doctor gave Mr. Haines a flu shot—a vaccine to prevent *influenza*.
monsoon *(n)* mon-SOON	Dutch	a seasonal wind of the Indian Ocean and southern Asia	The *monsoon* brought heavy rainfall to the Indian coast.
portfolio *(n)* pawrt-FOH-lee-oh	Italian	a flat, portable case for carrying papers, drawings, or photos	The artist removed several illustrations from her *portfolio* and placed them on the desk.
rendezvous *(n)* RAHN-day-voo	French	an appointment to meet at a set place or time	The four men arranged a secret *rendezvous* in another city to discuss their plot to overthrow the king.
sentinel *(n)* SEN-tn-l	Italian	a person who stands guard or keeps watch	*Sentinels* patrolled the bridge, on the lookout for enemy soldiers.
suite *(n)* sweet	French	a group of connected rooms making up one unit	The senator and her family occupied a two-room *suite* at the hotel.
tariff *(n)* TAR-if	Arabic	a government tax on imports or exports	Imposing a *tariff* on an imported product increases the cost of the item to the consumer.
tundra *(n)* TUHN-druh	Russian	vast, treeless plain of the arctic regions	The soil beneath the *tundra* remains frozen because the climate is so cold.
tycoon *(n)* tie-KOON	Japanese	a wealthy and powerful businessperson	The banker's successful investments made him a real estate *tycoon*.

Did You Know?

Just as English has borrowed from other languages, so have other languages borrowed from English. In fact, English words appear in most languages of the world, in either their original or a changed form. Japanese, for example, has its own version of such English words as *television* (*terebi*), while France has borrowed *tennis*, *sandwich*, and many other English words.

Own It: Develop Your Word Understanding

Think Fast

Directions: In this activity, you'll mingle with classmates—two minutes at a time! Here's what to do:

1. Your teacher will assign you a vocabulary word. Write it at the top of a sheet of paper. Then grab a pencil, stand up, and get ready to mingle.

2. Your teacher will announce, "Start." You have two minutes to pair up with a classmate and, together, write a logical sentence using both of your vocabulary words.

3. After two minutes, your teacher will call time. Quickly, write the sentence you composed (if you haven't already). If the sentence seems illogical, or you were unable to write a sentence, make a note of that.

4. Then get ready to go again—and pair up with someone different next time.

5. When the activity is over, hand in your sentences *or* exchange them with a classmate for evaluation, as your teacher directs.

Link It: Make Word-to-World Connections

Now and Later

Directions: In this activity, you'll think about words you're learning now and how these words may come in handy later. Pair up with a classmate, and follow these steps:

1. One of you reads the first vocabulary word aloud. Together, make sure that you understand the meaning of the word.

2. On a sheet of paper, write the word. Then write an example of when or how you might use this word in the future.

3. Repeat steps 1 and 2 for each word in the list.

4. In a class discussion, share some of your results. Point out any words that you don't see yourself using in the future—and prepare to be surprised and informed by how others *do* plan to use the words!

Master It: Use Words in Meaningful Ways

Your Choice

Directions: In this activity, you'll choose *one* of the following topics to write about. When you're finished, give a copy to your teacher. He or she will collect everyone's writing in a folder. When you have spare time in class, pull out someone's work, sit back, and enjoy a good read.

Writing Topics

(pick one)

> Write a skit in which one person proposes marriage to the other. Use the word *fiancé* or *fiancée* (or both words).
> Write an encyclopedia entry about the Spanish flu *or* bird flu. Use the word *influenza*.
> Write a poem about a person or animal caught in a *monsoon*.
> Record and write down an interview with someone about a *portfolio* of fashion designs, artwork, photographs, or written work.
> Write a short story about a *rendezvous*.
> Write an article about the *sentinel* tank used in war.
> Write a vacation brochure advertising guest *suites* near a specific destination. (You choose the destination.)
> Write an encyclopedia entry about the Boston Tea Party. Use the word *tariff*.
> Write a science report on a plant or animal that thrives in a *tundra*.
> Write a biographical report on a *tycoon*.

Vocabulary Mini-Lesson: Words Come from Mythology

Besides foreign languages, another interesting source of English words is Greek and Roman mythology. Mythology is the collection of myths, or stories that were told and written to explain how or why things were created. These stories usually involve gods and heroes.

Many familiar words have their origin in people or creatures described in ancient myths. For example, the word *martial* (of or relating to war or fighting), as in *Jose is studying martial arts*, comes from Mars, the Roman god of war.

Words to Know: Vocabulary Lists and Activities

In this section, you'll learn ten words that come from Greek and Roman myths. You'll learn the myths from which these words have arisen, as well as the more modern uses of the words.

List 15 Words from Mythology

Read each word, its origin, what it means, and how it's used.

Word	Its Origin	What It Means	How It's Used
Achilles' heel (n) uh-KIL-eez heel	*Achilles* was a Greek warrior whose only vulnerable spot was his heel.	a vulnerable point; weak spot	Consuelo generally eats a healthy diet, but her love of chocolate is her *Achilles' heel*.
atlas (n) AT-luhs	In Greek mythology, *Atlas* was forced to hold the heavens on his shoulders.	a book of maps	To locate Brazil, John looked at a map of South America in an *atlas*.
fauna (n) FAW-nuh	from *Fauna*, the sister of Faunus, the Roman god of animals	the animals of a region, time period, or other group	In science class, we studied the *fauna* of Africa, including elephants and zebras.
flora (n) FLOHR-uh	from *Flora*, the Roman goddess of flowers	the plant life of a region, time period, or other group	The *flora* of Tuscany, Italy, includes cypress trees and beautiful sunflowers.
mentor (n) MEN-tawr	In Greek mythology, *Mentor* was a friend and adviser of Odysseus (leader in the Trojan War) and teacher of his son.	a trusted adviser or teacher	During his first year on the job, Nico's supervisor became his *mentor*.
mercurial (adj) mer-KYOOR-ee-uhl	*Mercury* was a Roman god associated with swiftness, cleverness, eloquence, and various other qualities.	quick; active; eloquent; clever	Delia was a *mercurial* young girl who fluttered around the classroom like a butterfly.
odyssey (n) OD-uh-see	The *Odyssey* is a Greek epic poem about Odysseus's wanderings after the Trojan War.	a long series of wanderings or travels	The travelers' year-long *odyssey* across America began in New Jersey.
plutocracy (n) ploo-TOK-ruh-see	*Pluto* was the Roman god of the underworld and of wealth.	rule by the wealthy	In social studies class, we studied the difference between a *plutocracy* and a true democracy.
stamina (n) STAM-uh-nuh	From *stamen warp*, the thread of life spun by the Fates	endurance or staying power; the ability to last through a stressful effort or activity	Drinking plenty of water and having a nutritious snack will help give you enough *stamina* to get through the morning's exams.
zeal (n) zeel	From *Zelos*, the Greek god of eager desire	eagerness and excitement about something	Cara always spoke with energy and *zeal* about her favorite hobby, scuba diving.

Own It: Develop Your Word Understanding

Yes, It Is—No, It's Not

Directions: Work with a partner to complete the activity. For each organizer, complete these steps:

1. *What It Is:* In this box, state what the key word means in your own words.

2. *What It's Not:* List antonyms, expressions with an opposite meaning to the key word, or things/ideas that someone may confuse with the key word. For example, an *Achilles' heel* is not a strength; a *mentor* is not an enemy.

3. *Examples:* List examples of the key word. For instance, name your Achilles' heel; write an example of a friend's mercurial behavior.

4. *Memory Cue:* Sketch a simple illustration to help you remember the word's meaning.

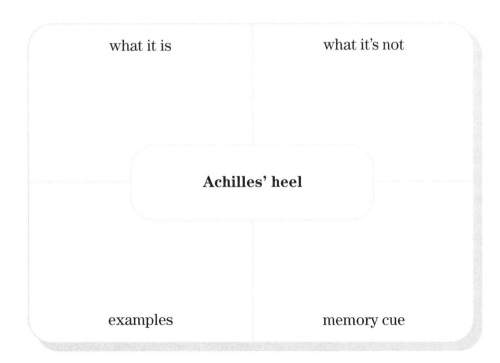

what it is   what it's not

atlas

examples   memory cue

what it is   what it's not

fauna

examples   memory cue

what it is

what it's not

flora

examples

memory cue

what it is

what it's not

mentor

examples

memory cue

what it is   what it's not

mercurial

examples   memory cue

what it is   what it's not

odyssey

examples   memory cue

what it is   what it's not

plutocracy

examples   memory cue

what it is   what it's not

stamina

examples   memory cue

what it is   what it's not

zeal

examples   memory cue

My swim coach has a
mercurial temper... one day he's calm,
and the next day he's furious at us and
says we don't work hard enough. Luckily, I
have enough zeal for the sport that it doesn't
bother me—I'd love it no matter what—and
I have lots of stamina to get through
the meets and the shouting.

Link It: Make Word-to-World Connections

Visiting Celebrity

Directions: Imagine that Achilles, Atlas, Fauna, Flora, Mentor, Mercury, Odysseus, Pluto, or Zelos is coming to visit your school. What do you think this "celebrity" would say to students? What might be the purpose for the visit?

Create a poster announcing the upcoming visit of one of these characters. The purpose of your poster is to inform students of the character's visit, the purpose of the event, and why students will want to attend. As an added challenge, on your poster use the vocabulary word that is derived from the character's name.

When your poster is finished, display it in your classroom.

Master It: Use Words in Meaningful Ways

That Was Then. This Is Now.

Directions: If myths were written about modern-day people, who would be the hero with one fatal weakness? Who would hold up the heavens? Who would give out sage advice, and who would be clever and eloquent? Who would wander the world after a major conflict?

Choose one of these nine mythological characters (Achilles, Atlas, Fauna, Flora, Mentor, Mercury, Odysseus, Pluto, or Zelos) and identify a modern-day person who is similar. Write a three-paragraph essay in which you—

> introduce the Greek character and the modern-day person and tell how they are similar

> tell how the Greek character inspired the modern-day vocabulary word

Vocabulary Mini-Lesson: Words Are Named After People and Places

Did you know that word *saxophone* comes from Antoine *Sax*, the 19th-century Belgian instrument maker who invented it? Such a word that comes from, or is based on, the name of a real or imaginary person is called an **eponym**. *Watt*, named for Scottish engineer James Watt is another example, as is *sandwich*, named for the Earl of Sandwich, the 18th-century English nobleman who invented it.

Many other common words get their names from people and places. Some are obvious—like *Morse code*, named for its American inventor, Samuel Morse. Others may surprise you. In List 16, you'll learn ten of these words.

List 16   Words from the Names of People and Places

Read each word, what it means, its origin, and how it's used.

Word	What It Means	Its Origin	How It's Used
braille *(n)* breyl	a system of writing and printing for blind people that uses characters made up of raised dots, which are read through finger touch	named after Louis Braille (1809–52), the blind French teacher who created it	Jeremy went to a special school to learn how to read *braille*.
decibel *(n)* DES-uh-bel	unit for measuring the loudness of sound (one-tenth of a bel)	Bel was named after Alexander Graham Bell (inventor of the telephone). The more common unit is decibel (the Latin prefix *decis* means "one-tenth").	Sounds exceeding 85 *decibels* can permanently damage your hearing.
guillotine *(n)* GIL-uh-teen	a machine for beheading by means of a heavy blade dropped between two vertical posts	named for Joseph Guillotin (1738–1814), a French doctor who proposed its use for executions	The last execution by *guillotine* occurred in Marseilles, France, in 1977.
leotard *(n)* LEE-uh-tahrd	a close-fitting one-piece garment worn by dancers and acrobats	named for Jules Léotard, a 19th-century French acrobat who designed the garment	All the dancers in the show wore black *leotards*.
marathon *(n)* MAR-uh-thuhn	a footrace of 26 miles, 385 yards	named for a Greek soldier's legendary run from Marathon, Greece, to Athens, to announce his country's battle victory	The Boston *marathon* is a race that attracts runners from all over the world.
mogul *(n)* MOH-guhl	A very wealthy or powerful person, especially a businessperson	comes from the Great Mogul, Mongol emperor of India in the 1500s	Joe's uncle is a business *mogul* who achieved great success in the automobile industry.
nicotine *(n)* NIK-uh-teen	a poisonous substance found in tobacco leaves, roots, and seeds	named after Jean Nicot, a French diplomat who introduced tobacco into France about 1561	The *nicotine* contained in cigarettes is harmful to smokers.
pasteurize *(v)* PAS-chuh-rize	to heat to a high temperature for a set period of time in order to destroy bacteria	named after Louis Pasteur (1822–1895), the French chemist who devised the process	*Pasteurizing* milk helps to prevent the spread of diseases.
ritzy *(adj)* RIT-see	From the Ritz hotels, known for their showy style and luxuriousness	extremely fancy or stylish	My cousin's sweet sixteen party was a *ritzy* affair at a fancy restaurant.
volt *(n)* vohlt	a unit for measuring electrical power	named for Italian physicist Alessandro Volta (1745–1827)	A lightning strike can discharge millions of *volts* of electricity.

Own It: Develop Your Word Understanding

Look It Up!

Directions: Work with a partner to complete the activity. Here's what to do:

1. Look up each vocabulary word in an encyclopedia, dictionary, or other reference source. Your goal? Find out something about each word that is not printed in the table in this book. For instance, you may find a braille alphabet, a picture of a guillotine, or a report on noise levels (in decibels) at a rock concert.

2. Fill in the table by writing and/or drawing a piece of new information about each word.

3. In a class discussion, share some of the facts you learned.

Key Word	Something New I Learned About This Word
braille	
decibel	
guillotine	
leotard	
marathon	

continued

mogul	
nicotine	
pasteurize	
ritzy	
volt	

Link It: Make Word-to-World Connections

It's All in Your Head

Directions: Work with a partner to complete the activity. Here's what to do:

1. Read the headings in the table on the next page.
2. Your partner reads each vocabulary word aloud. After you hear each word, write it in one of the columns in the table.
3. Repeat step 2. This time, you read the words aloud to your partner.
4. Compare lists. Talk about when you have heard these words before and how you have used them. Read the words in the first column aloud to help them become more familiar.

5. Finally, fill in the bottom section of the table. Based on your work with your partner, write ideas for when or how you could use some or all of the vocabulary words. Continue on separate paper if necessary.

This word is new to me in this lesson.	I have heard this word, but I've never used it.	I have used this word.

Here's how I plan to use some of these words:

Master It: Use Words in Meaningful Ways

So You Want To . . .

Directions: Write a guide for how to do something associated with a vocabulary word. For instance, you could write a guide called "So You Want to Learn *Braille*" or "So You Want to Train for a *Marathon*" or "So You Want to Power a Model Airplane with a 1.5-*Volt* Hobby Battery."

Make sure your guide gives clear, step-by-step instructions for how to accomplish a task. With this goal in mind, choose a task that is simple enough to "teach" in one or two pages of writing. Ask a friend to give your instructions a trial run to pinpoint trouble spots.

Give a copy of your guide to your teacher, who will collect them in a folder. When you have spare time in class, pull out a guide and read it. Make notes about projects that sound interesting. With all these ideas for things to do, you may never have another boring weekend!

Wrapping Up: Review What You've Learned

Here's a brief summary of what you've studied in this chapter.

> Many familiar words come from foreign languages. They have been added to English over the centuries and are still being added today. These words may not seem foreign, either because their form has changed or because we are so used to hearing them.

> Just as English borrows from other languages, so do other languages borrow from English.

> Words often trace their origin through two or more languages.

> Many words have their origin in people or creatures described in Greek and Roman mythology.

> Some common words are based on the names of people and places.

> A word that comes from, or is based on, the name of a real or imaginary person is called an *eponym*.

Flaunt It: Show Your Word Understanding

In the following exercises, you'll demonstrate your understanding of each vocabulary word. You will use vocabulary words, or forms of the words, to complete sentences and to write sentences of your own.

A Sentence Completion

Directions: Circle the letter of the word that best completes each sentence.

1. The soldier's regiment worked closely with other regiments in the _____.

   a. brigade   **b.** sentinel
   c. guillotine   **d.** marathon

2. Bill Gates, a cofounder of Microsoft, is a world-famous business _____.

   a. czar   **b.** tycoon
   c. atlas   **d.** cavalry

3. At the party, guests tossed colorful _____ into the air above the birthday girl and sang "Happy Birthday" to her.

   a. tariffs   **b.** croissants
   c. rendezvous   **d.** confetti

4. Since _____ can be transmitted by coughs or sneezes, you should cough or sneeze into a tissue or your sleeve to prevent the spread of germs.

   a. nicotine   **b.** monsoons
   c. influenza   **d.** Achilles' heel

5. This toy is powered by a nine- _____ battery, which is rectangular shaped.

   a. decibel   **b.** volt
   c. debut   **d.** debris

Word Bank

Directions: Choose two words from the box to complete each sentence. Write the words in the appropriate blanks. You will not use all the words.

Achilles' heel	czar	flora	odyssey
atlas	debris	guillotine	portfolio
boomerang	debut	leotard	rendezvous
braille	etiquette	mentor	ritzy
croissant	fiancé	mercurial	stamina

6. Dora and her _____ learned basic wedding _____, such as sending a handwritten thank-you note for each gift received.

7. The leather _____ contained a collection of poems printed in _____.

8. Would you like to become the _____ to a/an _____ yet lovable little boy who needs a big-brother figure?

9. On my _____ through the Outback, I collected such artifacts as a/an _____, an oilskin hat, and clapsticks (a type of musical instrument).

10. When my sister made her _____ in a dance production, she wore a/an _____ that she herself had designed.

 Writing

Directions: Write one or more sentences to answer each question. Be sure to use the vocabulary word, and write your sentences on a separate sheet of paper.

11 Which teacher in your school could help you with an *algebra* problem?

12. What is one type of office worker who is likely to work in a *suite* of offices?

13. If you were offered a free *tundra* vacation, how would you respond?

14. Why do dairy companies *pasteurize* milk?

15. What is one topping that you might find tasty on a *croissant*?

Activities à la Carte: Extend Your Word Knowledge

The activities on this page are presented à la carte, like items on a restaurant menu, meaning that you can choose from a variety of options. Your teacher may assign an activity or let you pick the one that tempts your appetite. If time allows, you might do more than one activity. All of the activities feature the same ingredient: **words derived from many sources**. Dig in!

My Eponym

If you could coin a new word based on your name, what would it be? What would this new word mean, and why would it derive from your name? Play around with your own name and those of your friends. Create a list of eponyms, complete with definitions. If you're enjoying yourself, create an entire class directory of eponyms.

E-Game

Use one or more vocabulary words to inspire your own electronic game. Write a game profile stating the purpose of playing (to become a shipping *tycoon*, to *rendezvous* with a military spy, to seek treasure in the arctic *tundra*, etc.). Also give information such as how many players, how many levels are in the game, and so on. Finally, sketch or otherwise create a sample "screen shot" of what the game will look like.

Word Associations

Choose a vocabulary word and make a poster of words associated with, or linked to, the key word. For instance, use *brigade* to inspire a poster that explains military terms and ranks. Use *croissant* to inspire a poster that introduces French foods. Useful information to include for each word is a pronunciation guide, a definition, and the etymology (origin). You may also want to include pictures, recipes, or other extras to lure readers.

Follow the Leader

Does Russia still have a *czar*? What are other titles of world leaders? Find out what heads of state are called in various countries around the world. Write the information on small notes and pin them to nations on a world map, or create another type of visual to share the facts with your class.

Yellow Pages

For a week, study your world for examples of modern uses of names from mythology. Look at brand names, company names (try the yellow pages in a phone book), signs, and billboards. Ask people for examples that they know of. Report back to the class and offer your answer to the question *Why do names from ancient myths remain so alive today?*

 ## English Without Borders

In this chapter, you learned some "English" words borrowed directly from other languages, such as *fiancé* and *suite*. Now turn the tables. Look for English words that are used in other languages. A librarian can help you start your search. Based on your research, make a list of ten key English words that all foreigners should know.

Telling Stories

Choose a Greek or Roman myth that younger kids would enjoy. Arrange with a teacher or librarian to present this myth to a group of kids. Practice telling or reading the myth aloud (you could research tips for reading aloud). If possible, prepare at least one visual such as a poster or illustrations to grab your listeners' interest. If you enjoy the spotlight, perhaps you are destined for a career as an entertainer, teacher, or public speaker.

One of a Kind—or One of Many?

Just how special are the words listed in this chapter? When people need to use the exact right word, do these words stand out as one of a kind? Or are they one of many equally useful choices? Develop your opinion on this issue by grabbing a thesaurus and looking up vocabulary words. Does each vocabulary word have synonyms? Are the synonyms equally precise, expressive, or unique? Overall, do you think English is richer because of words derived from other languages and proper nouns, or simply more cluttered?

Learning New and Special Words

6

We all live in the same world: planet Earth. However, we also occupy our own unique worlds, made up of personal experiences and knowledge. When we study specific subjects or pursue careers, we enter other worlds— the world of science or technology, for instance, or the medical or legal world. All of these worlds have specialized words associated with them. In this chapter, you'll learn words from some of these worlds, and you'll add words to the vocabulary of *your* world.

Objectives

In this chapter, you will learn

> How and why our language expands

> New words from technology, science, medicine, and law

Sneak Peek: Preview the Lesson

The Best of All Worlds

Think about your world and your language. When you're with friends and family, what words and expressions do you use that "the outside world" may not use? Write some of these words in the My World circle at the top of the next page.

Next, read the words in the outer circles. These are some of the words that you'll study in this chapter. If any of these words fit into your world, write them in the center circle as well. Chances are, your personal world already shares elements with at least one other world!

Vocabulary Mini-Lesson: How Our Language Expands

The English language is constantly growing and changing. New words are added, and old words take on new or changed meanings. Consider the word *surf*, for example. Originally, it was a noun, referring to the waves of the sea breaking against the shore. Then it became a verb, referring to the sport of riding the waves, as in "Get your board, dude, and let's go *surfing*!" Before long, some people were standing on sailboards and going *windsurfing*. Today, most people do their surfing far from water and wind: they use their computers to "surf the Web."

Sometimes new words are formed by blending other words. For example, *fantabulous* combines letters from *fantastic* and *fabulous*. *Sitcom* blends the words *situation* and *comedy*. Other words enter our language through technology and science, such as *Google*, *text messaging*, *high-definition*, *Internet*, and *wireless*.

Words to Know: Vocabulary Lists and Activities

The first two lists in this section contain relatively new words that came into being for various reasons, such as changes in technology and science, and trends in pop culture. The last two lists contain words that are often used in the specific areas of medicine and law.

List 17   Technology and Science Words

Read each word, what it means, and how it's used.

Word	What It Means	How It's Used
avatar *(n)* AV-uh-tahr	an electronic image that represents a person on the computer (usually during a game)	When I played the fantasy computer game, my *avatar* sort of looked like me, except that she was wearing a red princess's dress.
browser *(n)* BROU-zer	computer software used to access Internet Web sites	Use your *browser* to go to weather.com to find out the forecast for tomorrow.
clone *(v)* klohn	to make a copy of	Scientists have been able to *clone* sheep, pigs, cats, and other animals.
cookie *(n)* KOOK-ee	a small file or part of a file stored on a computer, containing information about the user	My library card number is stored in a *cookie* on my computer.
database *(n)* DEY-tuh-beys	a large collection of data organized for rapid search by a computer user	Peter searched the sports *database* for statistics about his favorite players.
GPS *(n)* gee-pee-ess	(short for *Global Positioning System*) a navigational system that uses satellite signals to track the user's position	Having a *GPS* receiver in your car makes it easy to find your way.
hacker *(n)* HAK-er	a person who illegally gains access to files in a computer system	Police arrested the *hacker* who had broken into the company's database.
nanosecond *(n)* NAN-uh-sek-uhnd	one billionth of a second	It took the computer only a few *nanoseconds* to perform the complex calculations.

continued

pixel *(n)* PIK-suhl	one of the tiny picture elements that together make up the image displayed on a video screen	Thousands of *pixels* create the picture that appears on a computer monitor.
virus *(n)* VIE-ruhs	a usually destructive computer program that produces copies of itself and inserts them into other programs without the user's knowledge	The *virus* that infected the company's computers wiped out important data.

Own It: Develop Your Word Understanding

Accept or Reject?

Directions: In this activity, you'll spot fake definitions of the vocabulary words. Here's how the activity works:

1. Your teacher will assign you and a partner one of the vocabulary words. On an index card, write your names and the word you received. On the back of the card, write two things: a *correct* definition of the word, and an *incorrect* definition that you make up. (Label each definition.) Try to make your incorrect definition close to the real one and not something absurd or far-fetched, so that the activity is more challenging.

2. Your teacher will mix everyone's cards together in a box.

3. Your teacher will pull out a card and read the vocabulary word aloud. Then he or she will read *one* of the definitions on the card. You must decide if the definition is correct or incorrect.

4. Your teacher will ask for a show of hands to see if you *accept* or *reject* the definition. Be ready to defend your vote!

Link It: Make Word-to-World Connections

Thinking of You

Directions: Technology and science words can seem intimidating, or scary, to people. Their fear can stand in the way of learning the new words. Do you know someone like this? Help this person by personally explaining a few technology and science words. Follow the steps at the top of the next page.

1. Review the list of vocabulary words. As you do so, think about someone you know who may be unfamiliar with some of these words. Choose *three* words to work with.

2. Write a letter to the person you chose. In the letter, mention that you are studying technology and science words. Suggest that this person may like to know about a few of these words. Then explain the meaning of each word and give an example of how the person might use it in his or her own life.

3. Share a copy of the letter with your teacher. Whether or not you send the letter to its addressee is up to you!

Master It: Use Words in Meaningful Ways

Have a Conversation

Directions: In this activity, you and your classmates will have a conversation with your teacher. The goal is to use as many vocabulary words as possible during the conversation. Here's how it works:

1. Your teacher will divide the class into teams.

2. Your teacher will get a conversation started by reading one of these prompts:

   > I wonder if having a home computer is a necessity or a luxury.

   > I wonder if any of these terms will become outdated in the next 20 years.

   > I wonder which of these things will have the biggest impact on the lives of people in this room.

3. Raise your hand to signal that you want to share in the conversation. Then state a sentence that uses a vocabulary word *and* that makes sense in the conversation. (A team gets one point for each word used correctly.)

4. When one or more conversations are finished, your teacher will add up each team's points and declare a winner.

List 18   New Words and Meanings

The first list contained words specifically from technology and science; here are some new words on a variety of other pop-culture and current topics. Read each word, what it means, and how it's used.

Word	What It Means	How It's Used
bling or **bling-bling** *(n)* bling	flashy or expensive jewelry or other possessions	All the performing artists showed off their *bling* at the awards show.
carjacking *(n)* KAHR-jak-ing	(blend of *car* and *hijacking*) the forcible taking of an automobile from its driver	The man who tried to force his way into the car was arrested for attempted *carjacking*.
cybercafe *(n)* SY-ber-ka-FAY	a coffee shop that provides computers for customers to access the Internet (The prefix *cyber-* means "relating to computers.")	While on vacation, we stopped at a *cybercafe* to send e-mails to friends back home.
grassroots *(adj)* GRAS-roots	starting or operating at the local level; involving ordinary citizens	The people formed a *grassroots* organization to work for the candidate's election.
hybrid *(adj)* HIE-brid	having two or more sources of power	Most *hybrid* cars have both gasoline and electric motors.
intranet *(n)* IN-truh-net	a network that functions like the Internet, but where access is restricted to certain people (such as employees at a certain company)	My teacher puts all of her handouts on the school *intranet*, so that they can be used by other teachers.
lurk *(v)* lurk	to read messages on an Internet chat room or other group without contributing	I didn't have anything to add to the Web group discussion, so I just *lurked* and listened to what other people had to say.
multitask *(v)* MUHL-tee-task	to perform two or more tasks at the same time	To carry out the many duties of this job, you must be able to *multitask*.
pescatarian *(n)* PES-kuh-TAHR-ee-uhn	a vegetarian who eats fish	My sister is a *pescatarian*—she doesn't eat any meat from land animals, but she does eat salmon, tuna, and white fish.
prequel *(n)* PREE-kwuhl	a movie or literary work about events that occur before those in another movie or work (This word contains the prefix *pre-*. See List 2, page 10.)	*Wide Sargasso Sea* by Jean Rhys is a *prequel* to Charlotte Brontë's novel *Jane Eyre.* It tells the story of Mr. Rochester before he came to England.

Own It: Develop Your Word Understanding

You and Your Bling

Directions: Write your answer to each question on the lines provided.

1. What are some examples of *bling* that you own—or wish you owned?

_____

2. Do you think *carjacking* is a suitable theme for a kids' electronic game?

_____

3. What are some reasons why a teenager would go to a *cybercafe*?

_____

4. Who is more likely to have a *grassroots* fan club: a band that is just starting out, or a band that has put out several albums?

_____

5. Why does a *hybrid* car have two motors?

_____

6. Give an example of a time when you *multitasked*.

_____

7. A *prequel* to a movie about a lunar (moon) colony might be about what?

_____

Link It: Make Word-to-World Connections

Career Paths

Directions: In a small group, discuss how each vocabulary word relates to one or more career paths. For instance how might *bling* relate to the careers of a jewelry designer, a movie star, and an advertising executive? How might *carjacking* relate to the careers of a lawyer, an insurance agent, and a police officer?

Use the organizer below to record links between vocabulary words and career paths. Then in a class discussion, explain some links that your group discussed.

Links Between Vocabulary Words and Careers

bling	carjacking
cybercafe	grassroots
hybrid	intranet
lurk	multitask
pescatarian	prequel

Master It: Use Words in Meaningful Ways

Crystal Ball

Directions: Gaze into your crystal ball at your future. Which career listed in the previous activity seems most suited to you? Do a little research to learn more about this career. A librarian can help you find books and Web sites on specific careers or skills. You can also interview knowledgeable people and read news stories and magazines.

Use your research findings to write a one-page summary of your chosen career. In your summary, use at least one vocabulary word. Your teacher will collect copies of everyone's summaries in a folder. When you have a few spare minutes in class, pull out a career summary and read it. Who knows? Your future may be in that folder!

Words to Know: Vocabulary Lists and Activities

Technology and science terms are not the only special words in our varied language. The fields of medicine and law are filled with words that people use in everyday conversation, hear on television and in the movies, and read in newspapers and magazines.

List 19   Medical Words

Read each word, what it means, and how it's used.

Word	What It Means	How It's Used
acute *(adj)* uh-KYOOT	sharp and severe	The runner had to stop because she had an *acute* pain in her side.
adrenaline *(n)* uh-DREN-l-in	a hormone that is released in response to stress, to help you get through it	When I saw that there was only one minute left in the game, I got a last-minute rush of *adrenaline*, and I worked hard to score a final goal.
blood pressure *(n)* bluhd PRESH-er	the pressure of the blood against the walls of the blood vessels, especially the arteries	The doctor warned Mr. Jensen that his high *blood pressure* could damage his heart.

continued

deficient *(adj)* dih-FIH-shunt	missing a necessary substance, quality, or element	Vegetarians have to be careful to make sure they don't become *deficient* in iron, a mineral most commonly obtained from meat.
diagnosis *(n)* die-uhg-NOH-sis	identification of a disease by studying its signs and symptoms	After carefully examining the patient, the doctor said that her *diagnosis* was pneumonia.
dislocate *(v)* DIS-loh-kayt	to put out of place, especially to move a bone from normal connection to another bone	Our team's pitcher *dislocated* his shoulder and had to sit out for the rest of the season.
fracture *(n)* FRAK-cher	the breaking of a body part	The passenger suffered several bone *fractures* in the car crash.
indigestion *(n)* in-di-JES-chuhn	discomfort resulting from difficulty digesting food	Eating greasy foods gives me *indigestion*.
metabolism *(n)* muh-TA-buh-lih-zuhm	the chemical changes within a body, including the buildup and breakdown of substances (often specifically used to refer to the breakdown of food and its transformation into energy)	Runners often have fast *metabolisms*, which allow them to eat extra calories without gaining weight.
preventive *(adj)* prih-VEN-tiv	devoted to or concerned with prevention, the avoidance of something (in medicine, specifically of disease)	Getting a flu shot was a *preventive* measure to help me avoid getting sick this winter.

Own It: Develop Your Word Understanding

Yes, It Is—No, It's Not

Directions: Work with a partner to complete the activity. For each organizer, complete these steps:

1. *What It Is:* In this box, state what the key word means in your own words.

2. *What It's Not:* List antonyms, expressions with an opposite meaning to the key word, or things/ideas that someone may confuse with the key word. For example, *acute* is not chronic. *Blood pressure* is not a heart rate.

3. *Examples:* List examples of the key word. For instance, give an example of a food that gives you *indigestion* or jot down a veterinarian's *diagnosis* of your pet's health problem.

4. *Memory Cue:* Sketch or write a clue to help you remember the word's meaning.

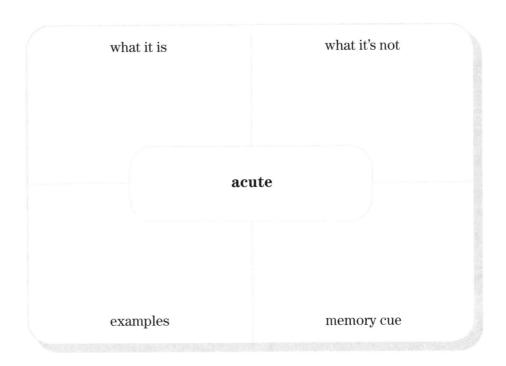

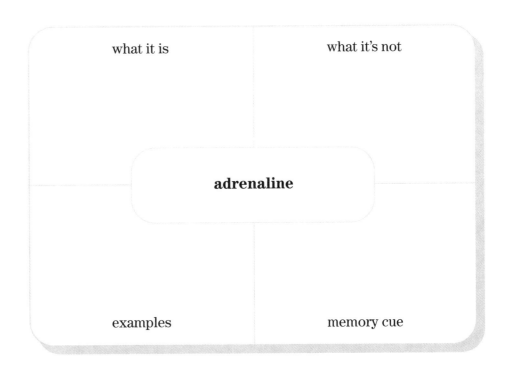

what it is

what it's not

blood pressure

examples

memory cue

what it is

what it's not

deficient

examples

memory cue

what it is   what it's not

diagnosis

examples   memory cue

what it is   what it's not

dislocate

examples   memory cue

what it is	what it's not

fracture

examples	memory cue

what it is	what it's not

indigestion

examples	memory cue

what it is	what it's not

metabolism

examples	memory cue

what it is	what it's not

preventive

examples	memory cue

> Yesterday afternoon, I had a bad case of <u>indigestion</u>. I should take <u>preventive</u> measures and not eat that mystery meat at the cafeteria anymore.

Link It: Make Word-to-World Connections

Asked and Answered

Directions: In this activity, you will ask a question about a vocabulary word *and* answer classmates' questions. Here's how the activity works:

1. Skim the list of vocabulary words and their definitions. What questions come to mind about one or more of the words?

2. On a slip of paper, write a question using one of the vocabulary words. For instance, you might ask, What does *indigestion* feel like? or How does a *dislocated* body part heal?

3. Give your question to your teacher, who will mix together all the slips of paper.

4. Your teacher will pull out a question and read it aloud. If you know an answer, raise your hand. For example, you might say, "*Indigestion* feels like hot bubbles that start in my stomach and go up my throat."

5. If your teacher reads a question and no one knows an answer, write the question down to use in the following activity.

Master It: Use Words in Meaningful Ways

Ask Me Again

Directions: Choose one unanswered question from the activity above and find an answer to it. You might choose to consult someone with medical knowledge, such as a school nurse, a pharmacist in a local drugstore, your family doctor, or a health teacher. Other sources of medical information include medical encyclopedias, health textbooks, hospital newsletters, and trustworthy Web sites such as that of the American Heart Association.

Based on information you find, write an answer to the question. Then read the question and your answer to the class.

List 20   Legal Words

Read each word, what it means, and how it's used.

Word	What It Means	How It's Used
alibi (n) AL-uh-bie	the claim or fact that a person was in a different place when a crime was committed and so could not have committed the crime	Ms. Whitmore's *alibi* is that she was at the movies with her cousin when the theft occurred.
convict (v) kuhn-VIKT	to judge or prove to be guilty of a crime	The lawyer insisted that there was more than enough evidence to *convict* the accused man.
copyright (n) KOP-ee-rite	the exclusive right to reproduce, publish, or sell an original work	Authors have the *copyright* to each work they create.
enact (v) en-AKT	to establish by legal authority (in particular: to make a bill into law)	The mayor will *enact* several new policies once he is sworn into office.
enforce (v) en-FAWRS	to carry out or cause to do forcibly	The police are responsible for *enforcing* the traffic laws.
fraud (n) frawd	intentional deception; trickery	Mr. Fiore was arrested for *fraud* when he tried to sell property that he did not own.
guardian (n) GAHR-dee-uhn	a person legally responsible for the care of another person	With Ricardo's parents in Mexico, Uncle Juan served as the boy's *guardian*.
illegal (adj) i-LEE-guhl	not legal; against the law	It is *illegal* to drive a car without a license.
lawsuit (n) LAW-soot	a case before a court	The actor filed a *lawsuit* against the magazine for printing a story that was untrue.
testify (v) TES-tuh-fie	to make statements sworn to be true in a court of law	The witness *testified* that she saw Mrs. Bernstein steal the money.

Own It: Develop Your Word Understanding

Mix and Match

Directions: In this activity, you will mingle with classmates, trying to match vocabulary words with their definitions. Here's what to do:

1. Your teacher will write each vocabulary word on an index card. On separate cards, he or she will write the definitions. Then the cards will be jumbled together in a box.

2. Pull one card from the box. You'll have either a vocabulary word or a definition.

3. Move around the classroom to find the person who has the definition of your vocabulary word, or the word that goes with your definition.

4. In a class discussion, explain how easy or difficult it was to make the match. Which words or definitions made you think hard about whether they were a correct match? Which were easier to eliminate?

Link It: Make Word-to-World Connections

Need an Alibi?

Directions: We often use legal words in nonlegal settings. For instance, your sister may state that it is *illegal* for you to touch her possessions, or a friend may *testify* against you when a third friend asks who's been spreading certain rumors.

In the first column of the table, give an example of how you could use each legal word in your everyday life. In a group, share your examples. Write other people's ideas in the third column.

Legal Word	Used in My Life	Ideas from Group
alibi		
convict		
copyright		
enact		
enforce		

continued

fraud		
guardian		
illegal		
lawsuit		
testify		

Master It: Use Words in Meaningful Ways

Long Arm of the Law

Directions: If you formed a student court of law at your school, how would it work? What *illegal* acts would be tried in your court? Who could be called to *testify*? Who would be the judge? The jury? What would happen if a student were *convicted* of an offense?

1. In a small group, brainstorm ideas based on these and other questions.

2. Together, prepare a description of the ideal student court of law. (To divide up the work, you can break the description into sections.) Be sure to use vocabulary words!

3. Present your recommendation to the class. You can use one spokesperson from your group, or take turns speaking.

4. Reflect on what you heard. How is your ideal court similar to those of other groups? How is it different? After hearing other ideas, would you change anything in your own court of law?

Wrapping Up: Review What You've Learned

Here's a brief summary of what you've studied in this chapter.

> Our language is constantly growing and changing. New words are added, while old words take on new or changed meanings.

> Some new words are formed by blending other words. Other words enter our language through technology and science.

> There are many medical and legal words that people use in everyday conversation, hear on television and in the movies, and read in newspapers and magazines.

Chapter Review Exercises

Flaunt It: Show Your Word Understanding

In the following exercises, you'll demonstrate your understanding of each vocabulary word. You will use vocabulary words, or forms of the words, to complete sentences and to write sentences of your own.

A Sentence Completion

Directions: Circle the letter of the word that best completes each sentence.

1. To find information on our country's first lady, use your computer's _____ to go to www.whitehouse.gov.
   - **a.** database
   - **b.** cookie
   - **c.** browser
   - **d.** GPS

2. In the nurse's office, Mrs. Jefferson put a cuff around Ethan's arm to get a reading on his _____.
   - **a.** adrenaline
   - **b.** indigestion
   - **c.** diagnosis
   - **d.** blood pressure

3. My dad, who is an accountant, filed a/an _____ against a client who refused to pay him for his work.
   - **a.** lawsuit
   - **b.** alibi
   - **c.** fracture
   - **d.** pixel

4. Last night, a _____ got into the school's main computer and opened some private student files.
   - **a.** virus
   - **b.** hacker
   - **c.** fracture
   - **d.** clone

5. C.S. Lewis published *The Lion, the Witch and the Wardrobe* in 1950. Five years later, he published a _____, *The Magician's Nephew*, set many years before *The Lion, the Witch and the Wardrobe*.
   - **a.** prequel
   - **b.** hybrid
   - **c.** fraud
   - **d.** copyright

B Word Choice

Directions: Underline the word that best completes each sentence.

6. Using a library's online card catalog, you can get a list of books on a specified subject in just a few (*blings, nanoseconds*).

7. If a jury agrees that a defendant is guilty, they must vote to (*convict, multitask*).

8. This movie is about a (*carjacking*, *guardian*) in a busy city, and the crime causes the main character's life to change in surprising ways.

9. It is (*hybrid*, *illegal*) to catch fish in this river without a fishing permit.

10. The patient is complaining of (*acute*, *grassroots*) stomach pain.

 Writing

Directions: Write one or more sentences to answer each question. Be sure to use the vocabulary word, and write your sentences on a separate sheet of paper.

11. Would you rather go to a library or a *cybercafe* to use a computer?

12. What kinds of *preventive* measures might you take to avoid getting sick?

13. Where would you look in a book to find the *copyright* information?

14. Would you find it easy or difficult to *testify* against a friend who had broken the law?

15. If you had the opportunity, would you *clone* a beloved pet?

Chapter Extension Activities

Activities à la Carte: Extend Your Word Knowledge

The activities on this page are presented à la carte, like items on a restaurant menu, meaning that you can choose from a variety of options. Your teacher may assign an activity or let you pick the one that tempts your appetite. If time allows, you might do more than one activity. All of the activities feature the same ingredient: **new and special words**. Dig in!

Do the Math

Math can help information come alive. If you enjoy charting statistics, drawing pie charts, or finding percentages, then grab a pencil! Choose a research topic inspired by a vocabulary word (percentage of your classmates who have ridden in a *hybrid* car, the gross earnings of various movie *prequels*, statistics on *fractures* that occur in school-related events, etc.). Do the research, do the math, and create a visual showing the results. Then share with your class.

Copycat

Find out about animals that have been *cloned*, such as Dolly the sheep or Dewey the deer. Create a Cloning Fact Sheet for your classmates, answering questions such as, What is a clone? What animals have been cloned? and What are pros and cons of cloning?

Your Pixels Are Showing

What is *pixel* art? Learn about this art form and find some examples of pixel art. In an oral report, share your knowledge and some examples of pixel art with the class.

Show-and-Tell

Do you miss the good old days of show-and-tell, back when you were little? Well, it's time to revive that practice. Your assignment? Bring in a *person* to show and tell about. This person must be connected in some way to one or more vocabulary words in this chapter. Perhaps you can introduce your class to an Emergency Medical Technician, a lawyer, or a Web-page designer. (Review class work for the Crystal Ball activity on page 119 for more ideas.)

Rock My World

If you are musically inclined, set some words from this chapter to music. You can rock them, rap them, croon them, chant them, or give them the blues. It's up to you!

Mock Trial

Did you enjoy the Long Arm of the Law activity in this chapter (page 129)? Get some friends together and stage a mock trial. Use ideas from the activity to give structure to your trial. You can use the trial to draw attention to a rule at school that you think is necessary—or ridiculous.

Is a cookie *una galleta*?

If you know a second language, search that language for new words and meanings. Can you identify new words in that language that don't have English translations? Or old words that have taken on new meanings? What about the new words and meanings in this chapter—do any of them translate into the other language and keep the exact same meaning? Use your findings to draw conclusions or make predictions about the two languages.

Brave New World

Did your study of new and specialized words spark an interest in a world outside your own? Find a way to explore this world. You could interview a professional, research articles and books, watch a video, or read news coverage. Based on your findings, prepare an oral report for your class. Your purpose is to persuade classmates that this world has a place for them in it.

A Suitcase Full of Words

At the beginning of this chapter you learned two blended words: *fantabulous* (*fantastic* + *fabulous*) and *sitcom* (*situation* + *comedy*). The formal name of blended words is **portmanteau** (port-man-TOE) words. *Portmanteau* is the French word for "suitcase"—just as you put different items together in a suitcase, you can put different items (words and word parts) together to make a new word. Some familiar portmanteau words are *brunch* (*breakfast* + *lunch*), *smog* (*smoke* + *fog*), and *motel* (*motor* + *hotel*).

Find ten more portmanteau words (Google "portmanteau words") and write them in a list. Trade lists with a partner and try to tell what smaller words make up his or her portmanteau words and what the new words mean.

Learning Words from Context

7

H ave you ever shared a big laugh with friends and then later tried to tell someone about it? And this person just stared blankly, as if to say, "What's so funny?" You may have responded, "Well, I guess you had to be there." What you realized was that the *context* of the conversation had something to do with its humor.

Just like spoken words, written words depend on context for full and accurate meaning. In this chapter, you'll study types of context clues commonly found in sentences and paragraphs. You'll learn to use these context clues to determine the meanings of unfamiliar words. You may want to add some of the fascinating words you study to your permanent vocabulary.

Objectives

In this chapter, you will learn

> How context clues can help you determine the meanings of unknown words

> Six ways to use context clues

> Words from literature, science, and history passages that you'll figure out yourself

Sneak Peek: Preview the Lesson

Appetizer

As you may know, an *appetizer* is a small sampling of food that whets your appetite for the meal to follow. Grab a partner and complete this lesson "appetizer" activity together.

First, one person skims the word lists in this chapter and reads some words aloud. Ten words is a good number to work with. (The lists are on pages 144, 150, 156, and 161.)

As your partner reads each word, record it in the appropriate column below. Return the favor by skimming the word lists and reading ten words aloud for your partner.

Finally, complete the sentence at the bottom of the table.

I have used this word.	I have heard this word but not used it.	This word is totally new to me.

In some of the passages in this chapter, I predict that I'll read about . . .

Vocabulary Mini-Lesson: How to Use Context Clues

As you're reading, you may come upon a word whose meaning you're not sure about. An author may use descriptive words that are new to you or whose meaning you've forgotten. Or an article on the Internet or in a magazine may contain unfamiliar scientific terms. In situations like these, context clues can help you figure out the meaning of the unknown words.

Context means the words or sentences that come before and after a particular word. The word *context* comes from the Latin word *contexere*, meaning "to weave together." Notice that it contains the prefix *con-*, which you learned in Chapter 1 (page 5).

Sometimes you need very little context, maybe just a phrase, to figure out a word. Other times, you may have to consider a whole paragraph to find the clues needed to understand a word's meaning.

Let's look at an example of how context clues work. Imagine that you hear this news story on TV:

Searchers today found the lost camper wandering through the Maine woods. After nearly a week with little or no food, the young man appeared pale and gaunt. However, he was in good spirits and told his rescuers that he was looking forward to eating a hot meal and sleeping in a real bed.

The word *gaunt* may be unfamiliar to you. However, you know that the young man has been lost in the woods for "nearly a week with little or no food" and that he is "looking forward to eating a hot meal and sleeping in a real bed." From these context clues, you can figure out that a person who appears *gaunt* looks thin and worn-out.

Context clues take various forms. For example, a writer may make a word's meaning clear by giving examples. Or the writer may provide a definition or explanation of a term, as in a science textbook. Sometimes a writer suggests the meaning of a word by making a comparison. You'll see examples of all of these kinds of context clues and others in the following sections.

Six Ways to Use Context Clues

1. Examine the Descriptive Details

The details that a writer includes when describing something offer important clues to word meaning. Notice the descriptive details in the following passage. Can you figure out the meaning of the underlined word from these details?

The sudden thunderstorm sent swimmers and sunbathers running for shelter. Towels, bags, and blankets were quickly snatched up, and chairs were hastily dragged through the sand. Before long, the beach was <u>desolate</u>. Not a single person remained.

Descriptive details tell you the meaning of *desolate*. Swimmers and sunbathers ran from the beach, taking their belongings with them. "Not a single person remained." Based on these context clues, you can conclude that *desolate* means "deserted."

On the next page is another example. What descriptive details help you figure out the meaning of the underlined word in this passage?

Some of the animals at the zoo seem almost as smart as people. My favorite monkey, for example, likes to <u>mimic</u> every movement I make. When I raise a hand, he raises a hand. When I jump up and down, he jumps up and down. Today I gave him a thumbs-up sign, and he gave it right back to me!

List three descriptive details that provide clues to the meaning of *mimic*.

a. _____

b. _____

c. _____

Based on the context clues you listed, what do you think mimic means? Write an explanation or definition.

_____

2. Look for an Explanation or Definition

Writers often explain or define a word when they use it. Look at these examples. What does the underlined word mean? How do you know?

Many people enjoy fishing from the <u>jetty</u>. You can see them sitting or standing on the stone wall that stretches out from shore into the water.

Based on the description in the second sentence, what do you think a *jetty* is?

_____

_____

After Kayla injured her eye playing soccer, she consulted with an <u>ophthalmologist</u>, a doctor who specializes in treating the eyes.

Based on the definition in the sentence, you can tell that an *ophthalmologist* is a doctor who _____

3. Search for Examples

Looking at the examples a writer gives can help you understand the meaning of an unfamiliar word. The examples may appear in the same sentence as the word or in a separate sentence.

> **Tip**
>
> When writers give examples, they often use these words:
>
> *for example   for instance   such as   including*

Read the following sentence. It uses examples as clues to the meaning of *crustaceans.*

Crustaceans, such as crabs, shrimp, and lobsters, have a hard shell and usually live in the water and breathe through gills.

What examples in the sentence help you figure out the meaning of *crustaceans?*

a. _____

b. _____

c. _____

Based on the examples in the sentence, what do you think a *crustacean* is? Write an explanation or definition.

_____

_____

Now look at another passage that uses examples as context clues.

Politicians are always creating new political slogans. Some are hard to forget, such as Franklin D. Roosevelt's "We have nothing to fear but fear itself." Another famous one is Theodore Roosevelt's "Speak softly and carry and big stick."

What examples does the writer provide that help you figure out what a *slogan* is?

a. _____

b. _____

Based on the examples, what do you think a *slogan* is? Write an explanation or a definition.

_____

_____

4. Look for Synonyms

A **synonym** is a word that means the same or almost the same as another word. For example, *huge* is a synonym of *enormous*, and *rapid* is a synonym of *swift*. Synonyms can be helpful context clues.

Look at the following examples. Can you find the synonyms for the underlined words?

> Early this morning, our group went on an <u>excursion</u> into the mountains. We returned from our trip before nightfall.

What is a synonym of *excursion*? _____

Now that you know what *excursion* means, use it in a sentence of your own.

_____

_____

> The hurricane had destroyed the village, and the people's <u>anguish</u> was apparent. The government was determined to ease their suffering.

What is a synonym of *anguish*? _____

Now that you know what *anguish* means, use it in a sentence of your own.

_____

_____

5. Look for a Comparison

Writers may suggest a word's meaning by comparing one thing to another. Often, the comparisons use the word *like* or *as*.

To what is Kevin compared in the following sentence? How does this comparison help you understand the underlined word?

Uncle Kevin, who is as <u>burly</u> as a professional wrestler, moved the piano all by himself.

In the sentence, Kevin is compared to a _____.
How does the comparison help you understand the meaning of *burly*?

_____

_____

What do you think *burly* means?

_____

What comparison is made in the next sentence? Hint: Look for the word *like*. How does the comparison help you understand the underlined word?

"I made the team," Allison said <u>blissfully</u>, sounding like a child who had just won a trip to Disneyland.

In the sentence, Allison is compared to what?

_____

How does the comparison help you understand the meaning of *blissfully*?

_____

_____

What do you think *blissfully* means?

_____

6. Look for a Contrast

While a comparison shows how two things are similar, a contrast points out how they are different. Writers making a contrast often use one of these words: *but, however, although, unlike,* or *while.* Look at this example:

Juliet used to be lazy and careless about her work, but over time she has become a <u>diligent</u> student.

The word *but* signals that there has been a change in Juliet. She "used to be lazy and careless." By contrast, she is now *diligent,* meaning "hardworking and careful."

Here's another example:

Unlike the Arctic, where temperatures are <u>glacial</u>, our weather is warm.

Which word signals that the sentence will express a contrast?
_____

Which word expresses a contrast to *glacial*? _____
Based on the contrast expressed in the sentence, what do you think *glacial* means?

_____

Notice, too, that *glacial* and *warm* are antonyms. An **antonym** is a word that means the opposite of another word. Writers often use antonyms when they make a contrast.

Tip

When you encounter an unfamiliar word, combine your knowledge of word parts (Chapters 1–4) with your knowledge of context clues. The more hints to meaning you can find, the better able you will be to figure out the word.

Words to Know: Vocabulary Lists and Activities

Now you'll read a nonfiction and a literary passage, and you'll try using context clues to figure out word meanings. Then you'll check if your meanings are correct, and you'll study these new words.

Reading a Nonfiction Text

The following passage comes from a column in a newspaper. Read the passage. As you read, use context clues to try to figure out the meaning of the underlined words.

Too Much Cell Phone Use?

The cell phone has become both a blessing and a curse in modern society. While it does facilitate communication, it also makes communication more difficult. This may sound like a contradiction, but consider this typical situation.

Mr. and Mrs. Dayton are working parents. During the day, they call each other on their cell phones in the event that there is an unforeseen delay getting home. In this way, at least one parent is always able to take charge of dinner preparations.

The Daytons' teenage son Ben also has a cell phone, which he uses to keep in touch with innumerable friends. In fact, Ben has so many friends that the Daytons complain that their son spends far more time text messaging and talking with his buddies than he does interacting with his parents.

"That phone has become an appendage of yours," Mr. Dayton tells his son. "Like another hand or foot. We can hardly ever talk with you anymore, because your attention is always focused on that gadget. When you're not talking or texting, you're downloading music with the darn thing or else taking pictures!" he adds, his voice rising in frustration.

Similar scenes are played out across the country every night, leaving parents as well as teens searching for a <u>mutually</u> acceptable <u>compromise</u>, some way to make everyone happy.

Write your definition of each word on the lines below. Then compare your definitions to those in List 21.

facilitate _____

_____

contradiction _____

_____

unforeseen _____

_____

innumerable _____

_____

interact _____

_____

appendage _____

_____

gadget _____

_____

frustration _____

_____

mutually _____

_____

compromise _____

_____

List 21   ## Words from a Nonfiction Text

Read each word, what it means, and how it's used. Were your definitions correct?

Word	What It Means	How It's Used
facilitate *(v)* fuh-SIH-li-tayt	to make easy or easier	Making an outline will *facilitate* writing a report.
contradiction *(n)* kon-truh-DIK-shuhn	a statement that conflicts with itself; a denial	The statement *Fast runners move slowly* is a *contradiction*.
unforeseen *(adj)* uhn-fawr-SEEN	not expected	Getting a flat tire was an *unforeseen* problem on our drive into the city.
innumerable *(adj)* i-NOO-mer-uh-buhl	too many to be counted	*Innumerable* stars fill the night sky.
interact *(v)* in-ter-AKT	to act on or in relation with; deal with	The shy boy did not *interact* much with the other students.
appendage *(n)* uh-PEN-dij	an attached part of an animal or plant	The tail of a dog is an *appendage*.
gadget *(n)* GAJ-it	an electronic or mechanical device	This new *gadget* peels carrots automatically.
frustration *(n)* fruh-STRAY-shuhn	a feeling of annoyance; irritation	My *frustration* grew as I tried again and again to solve the impossible puzzle.
mutually *(adv)* MYOO-choo-uhl-ee	equally; jointly	Although the athletes were rivals, they *mutually* respected each other.
compromise *(v)* KOM-pruh-mize	means of agreement; settlement	The strike ended when both sides reached a *compromise*.

Own It: Develop Your Word Understanding

Share and Compare

Directions: Form a group of five people and assign each person two vocabulary words. For each of your two words, follow these steps:

1. **Compare definitions.** Compare the definition you wrote on page 144 with the definition given in the table above. If necessary, make corrections to your definition. To become familiar with this new word, read the passage again with the revised definition in mind.

2. **Identify context clues.** Look again at the context clues that helped you determine the word's meaning. Referring to the list at the top of the next page, identify the type(s) of context clues that helped you understand the word.

> ## Types of Context Clues
>
> > descriptive details
> > explanation or definition
> > examples
> > synonym
>
> > comparison
> > contrast
> > antonym

3. **Share and compare.** Practice saying your two vocabulary words aloud. Then share these words, along with your definitions, with your group. Point out the context clues that helped you understand the words. Finally, listen as others share their results, and make revisions to your definitions if necessary.

Link It: Make Word-to-World Connections

A Mile in Your Shoes

Directions: In the table below, you "visit" different places in your home and think about how vocabulary words relate to your life there. Answer the questions to express what it's like to "walk a mile in your shoes." Share your answers in a group or class discussion.

kitchen: Name three things that will *facilitate* cleanup after a meal.	**dining room:** What might a family member say that would cause you to state a *contradiction*?
front door: What guest's arrival was *unforeseen*?	**your room:** Among your possessions, which ones seem to be *innumerable*?

continued

family room: What is an enjoyable way to *interact* with a family member?

garden: What sharp *appendages* make roses hard to handle?

bathroom: What *gadgets* clutter your bathroom?

kitchen: Which kitchen chore causes you *frustration*?

dining room: What table manners have been *mutually* agreed upon by your family?

family room: How do you *compromise* to share possessions?

Today, our English teacher had us work in small groups to discuss the book **Lord of the Flies**. The members of my group <u>interacted</u> really well, and we came up with <u>innumerable</u> great insights about the characters. However, we were overcome with <u>frustration</u> when the bell rang and we didn't get a chance to share our ideas with the class.

Master It: Use Words in Meaningful Ways

Been There, Done That

Directions: Not everyone has a cell phone, but most people have at least one gadget in their lives. What *gadget* exists in your life? Does it cause *frustration*? Does it *facilitate* daily tasks? Does it cause *unforeseen* problems?

Write a one-page personal essay about a gadget in your life. Tell what it is and how it makes your life easier or harder (or both!). In your essay, use as many vocabulary words as are logical in the context of your topic. You can choose to write humorously or seriously. In addition, you are free to make up details to enhance your essay.

After you write your essay, read it aloud in a small group. Be prepared for some sympathetic groans, knowing looks, and laughter from your audience.

Reading a Fiction Text

The following passage comes from a short story. Read the passage. As you read, use context clues to try to figure out the meaning of the underlined words.

The Big Move

Unlike her younger brother, who was miserable at the thought of leaving the city, Madison was happy about the change. Instead of the <u>clamorous</u> racket of the city—car horns, sirens, shouts and screams—Madison <u>anticipated</u> the peace and quiet of the country. In her mind, she <u>envisioned</u> a <u>picturesque</u> town filled with trees and flowers, gentle breezes, and bright sunshine. However, although she was excited for a new location, there was one thing she worried about—the fact that she'd have to attend a new school.

At her school in the city, Madison was a <u>conscientious</u> student; she was responsible and always worked hard. She also excelled in a <u>multitude</u> of activities, such as figure skating and journalism. And Madison had a great group of friends, with whom she ate lunch every day. She was worried that things might become more difficult for her at her new school. What if the classes were more challenging? What if she had trouble making friends? What if she had to <u>pursue</u> new activities?

At her first day in the new school, Madison was <u>reluctant</u> to talk to other students. What if they didn't like her? But she managed to overcome her <u>apprehension</u> and introduce herself to everyone, and to her relief, they were all really nice. Within no time, Madison began feeling comfortable and getting into the <u>groove</u> of things—she learned where her classes were, she joined new activities, and she made close friends.

Write your definition of each word on the lines below. Then compare your definitions to those in List 22.

clamorous _____

_____

anticipate _____

_____

envision _____

_____

picturesque _____

_____

conscientious _____

_____

multitude _____

_____

pursue _____

_____

reluctant _____

_____

apprehension _____

_____

groove _____

_____

List 22   Words from a Fiction Text

Read each word, what it means, and how it's used. Were your definitions correct?

Word	What It Means	How It's Used
clamorous _(adj)_ KLAM-er-uhs	loud and noisy	The meeting turned into a _clamorous_ debate once the committee members began arguing with one another.
anticipate _(v)_ an-TIS-uh-payt	to look forward to; expect	Our family is _anticipating_ an enjoyable day at the beach.
envision _(v)_ en-VIH-zhuhn	to picture in the mind; imagine	Mr. Patterson likes to _envision_ himself as the head of the manufacturing division.
picturesque _(adj)_ pik-chuh-RESK	visually pleasing or charming	We vacationed in a _picturesque_ town on Cape Cod that had beautiful beaches and lovely gardens.
conscientious _(adj)_ kon-shee-EN-shuhs	very careful and exact	Sarah was a very _conscientious_ drama student; she spent hours reading her scripts and she worked hard on getting every line right.
multitude _(n)_ MUHL-ti-tood	a great number	Not getting enough sleep regularly can cause a _multitude_ of problems.
pursue _(v)_ per-SOO	to follow, especially in an attempt to reach a goal or result	If you want to _pursue_ your goal of becoming a chef, you should consider attending a cooking school after college.
reluctant _(adj)_ ri-LUHK-tuhnt	hesitant	I was _reluctant_ to try the vegetable stew that my mom made, but it turned out to be quite tasty!

continued

| apprehension *(n)* ap-ri-HEN-shun | the condition of being anxious or fearful of something | I stood on the edge of the diving board, filled with *apprehension* about leaping into the pool. |
| **groove** *(n)* groov | a fixed routine | At first, it was tough waking up at 6:30 A.M. to get to school, but after a while, I got into the *groove*. |

Own It: Develop Your Word Understanding

Follow the Clues

Directions: In this activity, you'll learn more about the value of— and possible shortfalls of—context clues. Follow these steps.

1. Scan the passage on pages 148–149, noting the context clues that helped you determine the meanings of vocabulary words. Then on a sheet of paper, list the words and the context clues. If you can't identify a context clue for a word, write "no context clue."

2. In a small group, discuss context clues. To get the conversation started, answer some of these questions.

> For which underlined words did you find context clues?

> Did any underlined words seem to have no context clues? If so, which ones?

> Did people in your group come up with different definitions for the same word? Why do you think this happened?

> Did context clues seem to mislead you about the meanings of any words? If so, explain.

> When using context clues to determine a word's meaning, what can readers do to make sure this meaning is accurate?

Tip: Using a Dictionary

When you come across a word you don't know, and you are unable to figure out its meaning from context, you may need to look it up in a dictionary. But dictionaries often show different forms of a word and give more than one definition. How do you know which definition is the one you need? Here are some hints.

> First, check the part of speech. For example, if the word in question is being used as a noun (the name of a person, place, thing, or idea), then look at the noun definitions.

continued

> Next, check the definitions given under that part of speech and see which one makes sense in the context of what you're reading.

Imagine you looked up **groove** from paragraph 3 of the fiction passage on pages 148–149. Which dictionary definition most accurately captures the meaning of **groove** as used in the passage?

Within no time, Madison began feeling comfortable and getting into the groove of things—she learned where her classes where, she joined new activities, and she made close friends.

> **groove** *(n)* **1** a long narrow channel **2** a fixed routine **3** good form **4** a pleasant rhythm
> **groove** *(v)* **1** to interact well with **2** to enjoy oneself greatly

The passage states that Madison got into the groove of things. Groove is used as a noun, to describe a state (specifically, a comfortable routine) that Madison was in. So the correct definition is "a fixed routine."

Link It: Make Word-to-World Connections

Person, Place, or Thing?

Directions: Follow these steps to complete the activity.

1. Read each word in the first column of the table below.

2. In the second column, complete the sentence *This word makes me think of* . . . by writing the name of a person, place, or thing.

3. In the third column, write a sentence or two explaining the connection. Try to use the key word in your explanation. A sample response for *clamorous* is completed for you.

This word …	…makes me think of …	Sentence
clamorous	my summer job	I once had a summer job in a *clamorous* office, where phones were always ringing and people were always shouting.

continued

This word . . .	. . . makes me think of . . .	Sentence
clamorous		
anticipate		
envision		
picturesque		
conscientious		
multitude		
pursue		
reluctant		
apprehension		
groove		

Master It: Use Words in Meaningful Ways

What Happens Next?

Directions: Reread the portion of the story about Madison on pages 148–149. Based on what has happened so far, what do you think will happen next? Write *one or two pages* telling the next part of the story. Use as many of the vocabulary words as you can. Then participate in a storytelling festival during which you and class-mates entertain one another with your tales.

Some helpful suggestions are included in the box on the next page.

Your Narrative Process

> To get your ideas flowing, have a brainstorming session with classmates.

> In your story, focus on *one* event, problem, or situation.

> You can focus on dialogue (conversation between characters) or action—or a mix of both.

> Ask yourself, What would this character do? Think? Say?

> Share a draft of your story with a classmate. Get feedback about what is interesting and what is confusing.

> Practice reading your story aloud at home before you read it aloud in class.

Reading a Science Text

The following passage is from a science article. Read the passage. As you read, use context clues to try to figure out the meaning of the underlined words.

All About Dolphins

Dolphins are fascinating creatures, closely related to porpoises and whales. Many people are familiar with the bottlenose dolphin, popular performers at shows in aquatic parks. However, the bottlenose is only one of some forty species of dolphins. Even the so-called killer whale is actually a member of the dolphin family.

Although dolphins are mammals, not fish, they are well adapted to underwater existence. Their streamlined bodies enable them to swim easily and rapidly. The dorsal fin, on the center of the dolphin's back, provides stability, while powerful muscles along the dolphin's back and tail help to propel the dolphin through the water.

Dolphins' eyesight is excellent, and they have highly developed hearing. To navigate underwater and locate objects, dolphins use echolocation, the same process that bats use to navigate in the dark. Echolocation enables the dolphin to determine the position of objects and prey through the <u>emission</u> of sound waves, which are reflected back to the dolphin as echoes.

A dolphin breathes through a single <u>blowhole</u>, a nostril in the top of its head, which is covered by a <u>muscular</u> flap. To breathe, dolphins contract this flap. When dolphins relax the muscles, the flap remains shut, creating a watertight seal when dolphins dive.

Dolphins live and travel in groups called <u>pods</u>. They are <u>carnivores</u>, or meat eaters. Some eat fishes, while others, like killer whales, also prey on seals, walruses, and other sea creatures. Typically, dolphins hunt in groups, although they may also hunt alone.

Scientists consider dolphins to be highly intelligent. They communicate through clicks, squeaks, and various other sounds. They also send messages through their body movements, such as <u>breaching</u>, or leaping out of the water, and hitting their tails against the water.

Write your definition of each word on the lines below. Then compare your definitions to those in List 23.

aquatic _____

_____

dorsal _____

_____

propel _____

_____

echolocation _____

_____

emission _____

_____

blowhole _____

_____

muscular _____

_____

pod _____

_____

carnivore _____

_____

breach _____

_____

List 23 Words from a Science Text

Read each word, what it means, and how it's used. Were your definitions correct?

Word	What It Means	How It's Used
aquatic *(adj)* uh-KWA-tik	occurring in or on water; relating to water	People vacationing at the beach often take part in *aquatic* sports.
dorsal *(adj)* DAWR-suhl	near or on the back	The scientist examined the *dorsal* scales on the snake's body.
propel *(v)* pruh-PEL	to move forward	Wind filled the sails, *propelling* the boat out to sea.
echolocation *(n)* ek-oh-loh-KAY-shuhn	the process of determining the position of objects by sending out sound waves, which are reflected back to the sender as echoes	Dolphins and bats use *echolocation* to navigate and hunt.
emission *(n)* i-MISH-uhn	something emitted or sent out	The *emission* of light from distant stars enables them to seen by astronomers.
blowhole *(n)* BLO-hohl	a nostril in the top of the head of certain sea mammals	A whale breathes through its *blowhole*.

continued

muscular *(adj)* MUHS-kyuh-ler	of, relating to, or consisting of muscle	The human *muscular* system enables the body to move.
pod *(n)* pod	a small group of animals, such as seals or whales	Marine biologists observed a *pod* of dolphins swimming alongside their boat.
carnivore *(n)* KAHR-nuh-vawr	a flesh-eating mammal	Dogs, cats, and bears are all *carnivores*.
breach *(v)* breech	to leap out of the water	When the whale *breached*, it nearly overturned the small fishing boat.

Own It: Develop Your Word Understanding

My Fellow Mammal

Directions: Answer each question in the left column by writing *yes* or *no* on the line provided. Then sort the vocabulary words (in *italics*): If you wrote *yes* next to a question, write the vocabulary word in Box A. If you wrote *no* next to a question, write the vocabulary word in Box B.

Based on these questions . . .

_____ **1.** Do you participate in *aquatic* activities?

_____ **2.** Do you use *echolocation* to find your way?

_____ **3.** Does your respiratory (breathing) system depend upon *emissions* to keep you alive?

_____ **4.** Do you breathe through a *blowhole*?

_____ **5.** Is your body *muscular*?

_____ **6.** Do you spend time in a *pod*?

_____ **7.** Are you a *carnivore*?

_____ **8.** If you were swimming in deep water, could you *breach*?

I can sort the vocabulary words like this:

Box A
(words that apply to dolphins *and* me)

Box B
(words that apply only to dolphins)

Link It: Make Word-to-World Connections

My Fellow Classmate

Directions: In a small group, explain your answers in the My Fellow Mammal activity on the previous page. Did everyone classify the words in the same way, or are there differences among students' work? If so, how do you account for the differences? If there are not differences, do you think there *could* be?

Summer is my favorite season. I love when the weather is warmer, and I get to do <u>aquatic</u> sports. I'm not the most <u>muscular</u>, so I can't <u>propel</u> myself through the water as fast as Michael Phelps, but I do my best!

Master It: Use Words in Meaningful Ways

I Can Explain

Directions: In this activity, you'll teach two vocabulary words to a group of classmates. Here's what to do:

1. Form groups of five people and assign two vocabulary words to each person.

2. On your own, figure out a way to explain your words to the group. Useful tools for explanation include these:

> *Make a comparison.* Compare a vocabulary word to something with which group members are already familiar. For instance, how is *echolocation* like the game of Marco, Polo?

> *Make a contrast.* Explain how a vocabulary word is opposite of, or unlike, something else. For instance, how does a *carnivore* differ from an *herbivore*?

> *Draw a visual.* Use your knowledge or a reference source to create a visual to *show* group members what something looks like. For instance, draw a picture of a dolphin as it *breaches.*

3. In your group, explain your vocabulary words. Listen as others explain their words, and jot down helpful memory cues.

Reading a History Text

The following passage comes from a history textbook. Read the passage. As you read, use context clues to try to figure out the meaning of the underlined words.

Ancient Egypt

There were two main classes of people in ancient Egypt. The upper class consisted of the pharaoh—Egypt's ruler—and the pharaoh's family, the nobles, and the priests. The lower class was made up of peasants. There also were a small number of artisans, or craftspeople, as well as merchants and scribes, who were responsible for writing things down. Foreign conquests added a third class of people—slaves. The thousands of peasants and slaves provided almost unlimited cheap labor for great public works.

Egypt was one of the few societies of the ancient world where women enjoyed rights nearly equal to those of men. Women could inherit and sell property without regard for the wishes of their husbands. Women were free to travel alone in public. The Egyptians also traced their ancestry, or family descent, through their mothers' families, not their fathers'. This view of family lines is known as *matrilineal*, which comes from Latin for "mother line."

The Egyptians believed in an existence after death, and spent much time preparing for this afterlife. They felt that, in order to be comfortable in the next world, people had to take along the things they had enjoyed on earth, or at least representations of these things. Their tombs, or <u>burial</u> chambers, contained everyday items, models of houses and ships, and paintings of scenes from daily life. All of these were to serve the dead in the next world.

According to the ancient Egyptians, each person has an <u>immortal</u> soul, which returns to the body after death. For this reason, they took great care to preserve the dead, especially the bodies of important people, by <u>mummification</u>. This process involved removing the internal organs and wrapping the body in linen treated with chemicals.

Write your definition of each word on the lines below. Then compare your definitions to those in List 24.

pharaoh _____

_____

artisan _____

_____

scribe _____

_____

ancestry _____

_____

matrilineal _____

_____

afterlife _____

_____

representation _____

_____

burial _____

_____

immortal _____

_____

mummification _____

_____

List 24   Words from a History Text

Read each word, what it means, and how it's used. Were your definitions correct?

Word	What It Means	How It's Used
pharaoh *(n)* FAIR-oh	a ruler of ancient Egypt	In ancient Egypt, the *pharaoh* was the head of government
artisan *(n)* AHR-tuh-zuhn	a worker skilled in a trade or craft; craftsperson	The crafts fair displayed beautiful wood and metal creations made by *artisans* from around the country.
scribe *(n)* skrahyb	a person whose job is to write down information	Recording historical events was the responsibility of the *scribe* in ancient Egypt.
ancestry *(n)* AN-ses-tree	line of descent; family descent; ancestors	Josh's family is of European *ancestry*.
matrilineal *(adj)* mat-truh-LIN-ee-uhl	tracing descent through the mother's family	A woman's ancestors have special importance in a *matrilineal* society.
afterlife *(n)* AF-ter-lahyf	existence after death	In some religions, people have a strong belief in an *afterlife*.
representation *(n)* rep-ri-zen-TAY-shuhn	an image; likeness	This scale model is a *representation* of an actual pyramid.
burial *(adj)* BER-ee-uhl	relating to the burying of a dead body	The field was set aside as a *burial* ground for warriors.
immortal *(adj)* i-MAWR-tl	living forever; everlasting	In Greek mythology, the gods were *immortal*.
mummification *(n)* muhm-uh-fah-KAY-shun	the process of treating a dead body with chemicals and wrapping it linen to preserve it	The ancient Egyptians preserved bodies through *mummification*.

Own It: Develop Your Word Understanding

Game Show

Directions: In this activity, you will be part of a game show team. When your team is "onstage" (in front of the class), the rest of the class will be your audience. They may clap, boo, or cheer as they watch. Here's how the game show works.

1. Assemble your team onstage. Choose one or two hosts, while the rest of you line up as contestants.

2. The host reads the definition of a vocabulary word. This is the *answer* to a question. If you know the *question*, raise your hand.

3. The host calls on the first person to raise a hand. This person asks the *question* that matches the host's answer. For instance, if the host read, "A ruler of ancient Egypt," then the correct question is, "What is a pharaoh?"

4. Each correct *question* wins a point. The game is over when each definition has been matched to the correct question. Finally, add up contestants' points to see who won.

Link It: Make Word-to-World Connections

New Contexts

Directions: When you read the passage on pages 159–160, you read each vocabulary word in the context of the topic people in ancient Egypt. In this activity, you'll choose a vocabulary word and put it into a *different* context. Grab a partner and follow these steps:

1. Toss around ideas for how you could put vocabulary words into different contexts. For instance, you could use *artisan* in a description of a crafts show. You could use *immortal* to tell about a vampire movie, or use *scribe* to specify the role of a club officer.

2. Based on your ideas in step 1, choose the word you would most like to work with.

3. Use your creativity to bring the word to life in its new context. A basic plan, for instance, is to write a paragraph. For added appeal, use graphics, music, costumes, or objects along with your written or spoken words.

4. Present your word in its new context to the class.

Master It: Use Words in Meaningful Ways

Seek and Find

Directions: In this activity, you'll choose a question from the list below and write a short report to answer the question. You'll need to do a little research. You may want to ask a librarian or teacher to recommend a nonfiction book about ancient Egypt. Other useful resources include history textbooks, biographies, and encyclopedias.

After you research and write your report, share it with a small group. After that, your teacher will sort the reports into folders, one folder per research question. When you have spare time in class, pull out someone's report and read it!

Research Questions

1. Who was one of Egypt's *pharaohs*? What is known about this ruler?

2. What did Egyptian *artisans* make? Did their work include *representations* of people? Animals?

3. What form of writing did Egyptian *scribes* use? (Include some examples.)

4. Give some facts about the *ancestry* of a famous Egyptian, such as Cleopatra. (Use the word *matrilineal.*)

5. What did ancient Egyptians believe about the *afterlife*? (Use the word *immortal.*)

6. What was the process of *mummification*? What did a mummified body look like?

Wrapping Up: Review What You've Learned

Here's a brief summary of what you've studied in this chapter.

> When you come upon a word whose meaning you're not sure of, context clues can help you figure out the meaning of the word.

> *Context* is the words or sentences that come before and after a particular word.

> Sometimes you need very little context to figure out a word's meaning. Other times, you may have to consider a whole paragraph.

> There are various kinds of context clues, including
>> descriptive details
>> explanations or definitions
>> examples
>> synonyms
>> comparison
>> contrast

> Combining your knowledge of word parts with your knowledge of context cles can make it easier to figure out the meaning of unfamiliar words.

Flaunt It: Show Your Word Understanding

In the following exercises, you'll demonstrate your understanding of each vocabulary word. You will use vocabulary words, or forms of the words, to complete sentences and to write sentences of your own.

A Sentence Completion

Directions: Circle the letter of the pair of words that best complete each sentence.

1. A cat's tail is quite expressive. When stalking prey, the cat may carry this _____ low and twitch the tip. If the cat _____ food or affection from humans, it may carry the tail high, like a banner.

   a. artisan, anticipates

   b. artisan, interacts

   c. appendage, anticipates

   d. appendage, interacts

2. In order to learn about Egyptian burial practices, I read about _____. I learned that the mummies of _____ such as King Tut and Ramses the Great have survived to today and have been studied by scientists.

   a. afterlife, pharaohs

   b. mummification, pharaohs

   c. ancestry, pods

   d. mummification, pods

3. When I decided to build a soapbox race car, the challenges seemed _____. But then I received some encouragement from friends and became determined to _____ my goal.

   a. innumerable, pursue

   b. picturesque, compromise

   c. clamorous, breach

   d. immortal, scribe

4. "The mouse-eared bat is a _____," the park ranger explained. "It eats insects that it catches while flying, and it eats insects such as beetles that it plucks from the ground. While flying, the bat locates insects and other airborne creatures using _____."

   a. contradiction, emissions

   b. contradiction, echolocation

    c. carnivore, emissions

    d. carnivore, echolocation

5. Kelsey won the grand prize in an art show for her painting of a dolphin as it _____. She said, "I was thrilled to enter the show, but I did not _____ winning the grand prize!"

    a. breached, facilitate

    b. apprehended, facilitate

    c. breached, envision

    d. picturesque, envision

B   Word Bank

Directions: Choose a word from the box to complete each sentence. Write the word on the line provided. Each word may be used only once.

interact	apprehension	gadget	mutually	aquatic
frustrated	representation	unforeseen	scribe	anticipate

Some people feel **(6)**_____ with new technology. When they are asked to use a new or complicated **(7)**_____, they panic. For one thing, they **(8)**_____ problems with learning to use the thing. A visual, such as a **(9)**_____ of the item with the parts labeled can be helpful—but just as often these drawings are confusing.

If you are comfortable with technology, why not offer your service as a "tech support" **(10)**_____? First, ask what is confusing the person. Write down the complaints. Then, identify problems that may be **(11)**_____ by the person, and write those down. Based on these notes, create step-by-step instructions and a trouble shooting guide. Your work will help the person **(12)**_____ with the gadget successfully.

Helping someone in this way can be **(13)**_____ beneficial, or helpful. For example, perhaps this grateful person can teach you to be a better swimmer and help you overcome your **(14)**_____ about trying **(15)**_____ sports. Bartering, or trading, services in this way creates two happy people!

 **Writing**

Directions: Follow the directions to write sentences using vocabulary words. Write your sentences on a separate sheet of paper.

16. Use *blowhole* in a description of a living creature.

17. Use *matrilineal* in a statement about tracing a family tree (ancestors).

18. Use *envision* and *picturesque* in the same sentence.

19. Use *unforeseen* and *frustration* in the same sentence.

20. Use *compromise* and *pursue* in the same sentence.

Chapter Extension Activities

Activities à la Carte: Extend Your Word Knowledge

The activities on this page are presented à la carte, like items on a restaurant menu, meaning that you can choose from a variety of options. Your teacher may assign an activity or let you pick the one that tempts your appetite. If time allows, you might do more than one activity. All of the activities feature the same ingredient: **context clues**. Dig in!

Curious George

Did a vocabulary word or reading topic in this chapter pique your curiosity? Learn more about it by designing your own research project. Your final product could be written, painted, programmed on a computer, filmed, or created in some other way. Include a glossary of key words and their definitions. Share your project with your teacher and with someone else who is curious.

My Own Personal Context

How does social context influence your word choices? For a week, be aware of how you talk in different situations—in a class, at a party, at a religious meeting, with a friend, with an enemy, and so on. Each day, record social contexts and key words that you used in each context. After a week, evaluate your lists and draw conclusions. Do you use the same vocabulary in all social situations? Or does it vary based on context?

Eavesdrop

Context clues can be a valuable tool in deductive reasoning. In this type of reasoning, you take general information and draw a specific conclusion from it. To try it out, eavesdrop on strangers' conversations. In a notebook, jot down odd bits of the discussions you overhear. Using clues in what you wrote down, make educated guesses about what the full conversations were about. Share some interesting results with your class.

Sling Some Slang

Many slang words carry meaning based on how they are used in a sentence—based on context, in other words. Brainstorm a list of slang words and expressions that you and your friends use.

Choose five of them that can have different meanings, depending on how they are used. Then write sentences showing at least two uses of each word or expression.

It's Greek to Me

If you have studied a second language, then you know what it's like to struggle to translate a sentence. You start with words you know and use those words as clues to the meanings of unfamiliar words. With a language-study group or your class, share some examples of how you learned new foreign words using context clues.

Track Five

For the next five days, keep track of new words you learn by studying context clues. Try to collect examples from all types of reading that you do—school assignments, magazines, fiction, messages from friends, and so on. After five days, you'll have a concrete measure of how much your literacy has increased.

The Survey Says . . .

Survey students about vocabulary and/or reading habits, and prepare tables or graphs of the results. First, develop three to five survey questions, such as, Do you plan to remember key words learned at school? or How often do you read for pleasure: once a day, once a week, once a month, or never? Survey a sampling of students. Then create data sheets showing the results. Report to your classmates—they may be surprised by what the numbers suggest.

Clue Review

Using context clues to determine word meaning can serve you well long after this lesson is over. With this in mind, create a poster-sized cheat sheet that lists and explains the types of context clues taught in this lesson. Use colorful paint or paper to make the poster eye-catching. Hang this clue review in your classroom or near a table where you normally do homework.

Thinking About Different Word Meanings

8

In a sense, words are like tools. As a writer, you choose the right tools to do the job. As a reader, you respond to how authors have used words to create meaning. With experience in reading and writing, you gain greater skill in using the tools of the trade: words.

This chapter offers you three types of tools to add to your toolbox. You'll learn about words with more than one meaning, literal and figurative uses of words, and descriptive words with precise meanings. Chances are, you'll recognize some of these words. Others will be new discoveries.

Objectives

In this chapter, you will learn

> Words that have more than one meaning

> Words that can be used literally or figuratively (in an expression)

> Words that have specific, not general, meanings

Sneak Peek: Preview the Lesson

Tools of the Trade

Take a look at some of the words you'll learn in this chapter. Which ones are familiar? Which ones are new to you? Which words seem so "foreign" that you can't imagine ever using them? Sort the words into categories, based on your responses. (You can put a word in more than one category.) After you complete the lesson, come back to this page and evaluate your progress in adding "tools" to your vocabulary toolbox!

Word List

compact	petrified	diverse	ambitious
profile	agile	colossal	fickle
beacon	summon	hardy	hostile

I've used this word.

I have not used this word.

I can't imagine ever using this word.

Vocabulary Mini-Lesson: Understanding Words with More than One Meaning

When you look up a word in a dictionary, you often find that the word has more than one meaning. Consider the word *file*, for example. How many meanings of this word can you think of? Compare the following sentences.

The secretary stores legal documents in a locked <u>file</u> at the office.

Before you turn off the computer, save the <u>file</u> you're working on.

Jeanine used a <u>file</u> to smooth her broken nail.

I'm going to add this chicken recipe to my <u>file</u> of favorites.

And these are just some of the *noun* meanings! There are other noun meanings, too, as well as several *verb* meanings.

While most words don't have as many meanings as *file* does, you may be surprised by how many words do have more than one meaning. You may also be surprised to find that many familiar words have less familiar additional meanings. For example, when you hear the word *duck*, you no doubt think of the bird that goes "quack." But did you know that duck is also a kind of cloth?

Words to Know: Vocabulary Lists and Activities

In this section, you'll study two lists of words with more than one meaning.

List 25   Words with Multiple Meanings

Read each word, its two or three possible meanings, and the sample sentences.

Word	What It Means	How It's Used
associate *(v)* uh-SOH-shee-ayt	**1.** to connect in one's mind	**1.** People *associate* springtime with birds and flowers.
	2. to spend time (with); join as a companion	**2.** Helena refuses to *associate* with selfish people.
compact *(adj)* KOM-pakt	**1.** closely and firmly packed together; solid	**1.** The soil was so *compact* that we found it difficult to dig a hole.
	2. arranged within a small space; occupying little space	**2.** In my *compact* kitchen, I can easily reach whatever utensils I need.
	3. brief and to the point; concise	**3.** The author has a *compact* style; he does not waste words.
conviction *(n)* kuhn-VIK-shuhn	**1.** act or result of proving (a person) guilty of a crime	**1.** Strong evidence against the accused man led to his *conviction*.
	2. strong belief	**2.** Because the senator spoke with such *conviction*, she was very persuasive.
culture *(n)* KUHL-cher	**1.** the customs, ideas, arts, and accomplishments of a nation or people	**1.** Art and music are important parts of Italy's *culture*.
	2. refined and educated ways of thinking, speaking, and behaving	**2.** Jacob is a man of *culture*, who appreciates fine art, classical music, and great literature.

continued

| digest (v)
di-JEST | 1. to change (food) into a form that the body can absorb | 1. Some people have difficulty *digesting* milk products. |
| | 2. to think over so as to fully understand | 2. The idea was so strange, it took me a while to *digest* it. |

Own It: Develop Your Word Understanding

Multiple-Meaning Mixer

Directions: In this activity, you will be given a vocabulary word *or* a definition. Your job is to find a classmate who has the corresponding vocabulary word or definition. Here's how the activity works:

1. Your teacher will fill a box with index cards. Each card will have either a vocabulary word or a definition written on it.

2. Take one card from the box.

3. Move around the classroom to find the person who has the word or definition that corresponds to what's written on your card. Since each word has more than one meaning, you'll form a group of three or four people.

4. With your group, review the multiple meanings of your word. Practice explaining the word's meanings in your own words rather than repeating the definitions in the book. Then write sentences that demonstrate the different meanings. (Write one sentence for each meaning.)

5. In a class discussion, take turns with members of your group to explain your word's multiple meanings, and read your sentences aloud.

Link It: Make Word-to-World Connections

Me, Myself, and I

Directions: In this activity, you'll choose *one* meaning of each vocabulary word to use in a description of yourself or your world. Follow these steps:

1. Each vocabulary word is listed in the table on the next page. Decide which meaning of each word best connects to your

life—to an experience you've had, for instance, or to a description of yourself or your community.

2. In the space beside each key word, explain which meaning of the word best connects to your life, and why.

3. Share some of your results with the class.

Key Word	Which Meaning of This Word Best Connects to Me and My World?
associate	
compact	
conviction	
culture	
digest	

Master It: Use Words in Meaningful Ways

Wanted: YOU!

Directions: Skim the following classified advertisements. Choose one that interests you and write a reply. You can be creative with your details and can make up information as needed. Be sure to use the italicized vocabulary word!

Finally, read your reply aloud in a small group in class. Explain whether you would answer a similar classified ad in real life.

Old Firehouse Teen Center

Classifieds

Reply to ads by submitting responses to Teen Center, Director's Office.

Needed: Workers to help design and build skate park, picnic area, and art wall. Compact piece of land has been donated. Labor to be provided by Teen Center.	**Selling:** *Compact*-sized motorcycle, suitable for teen with adult supervision. Red. New tires. Supply your own helmet. Will work with your budget.	**Available:** I specialize in organizing *compact* spaces. Closets, bedrooms, lockers, desk drawers—no task too small! Call me! I'll have you organized in a flash.
Needed: Weekend babysitter for 6-year-old boy. Must be able to prepare dairy-free snacks for child who has trouble *digesting* milk, milk products.	**Seeking:** Witnesses to thefts at the Teen Center. Information leading to *conviction* of thief/thieves will receive financial reward.	**Wanted:** Friendly, talkative teens who enjoy *associating* with the elderly. Fun volunteers needed for Senior Game Night at local retirement home.
Available: Math and science tutor. Do you *associate* math or science with failing grades? I can help! Evenings and weekends. Affordable.	**Welcome:** We are a group of teens who meet once a month to share and debate our *convictions*. Past topics include rules, morals, and spirituality. Join us!	**Wanted:** Artists to help create murals for two 100-foot outdoor walls. You suggest a *cultural* art style (Mexican, Native American, etc.).

List 26 Words with Multiple Meanings

Study this second list of words with more than one definition. Read each word, its two or three meanings, and the sample sentences.

Word	What It Means	How It's Used
foil *(n)* foil	**1.** a thin sheet of metal	**1.** Wrap the cookies in *foil* to keep them fresh.
	2. a person or thing that sets off the qualities of another by contrast	**2.** In this play, the humorous jester is a perfect *foil* for the serious king.
	3. a long, flexible fencing sword	**3.** The two opponents raised their *foils*, and the fencing match began.
outlet *(n)* OUT-let	**1.** a means of expression	**1.** Writing poetry provided a creative *outlet* for Jean.
	2. an opening or passage	**2.** The St. Lawrence River is the Great Lakes' main *outlet* to the sea.
	3. a receptacle into which an electric plug can be inserted to connect with a power supply	**3.** Plug your cell phone charger into the *outlet.*
profile *(n)* PROH-file	**1.** a side view, especially of a human face or head	**1.** I turned to the side, and the artist drew a sketch of my *profile.*
	2. a short, biographical description of a person	**2.** The magazine published a *profile* of our school principal.
recall *(v)* ri-KAWL	**1.** to bring back to mind; remember	**1.** David could not *recall* where he had seen the girl before.
	2. to request or order the return (of a product) to the manufacturer	**2.** The company *recalled* the tires because they had a dangerous flaw.
retain *(v)* ri-TAYN	**1.** to continue to have or hold; keep	**1.** Once steam radiators get hot, they *retain* their heat for a long time.
	2. to employ by paying a fee; hire	**2.** We *retained* a lawyer to represent us in court.

Own It: Develop Your Word Understanding

A Few Questions

Directions: Work with a partner to complete the activity. Follow these steps:

1. Divide the table so that one of you takes questions 1–6, and the other takes questions 7–12.

2. Answer the question in the first column of the table. Then, in the second column, write your own definition of the key word.

3. Share your answers with your partner. Help each other rewrite any definitions that were written inaccurately.

Question	My Definition of the Key Word, Based on Its Use in the Question
1. Do you store sandwiches in *foil* or plastic baggies?	**foil**
2. Among your friends, who could be called your *foil*?	**foil**

continued

3. Would you classify a fencing *foil* as a toy, a weapon, or sporting equipment?	**foil**
4. When you need an *outlet* for anger or sadness, what do you do?	**outlet**
5. At the entry to a neighborhood street, a sign says "No *Outlet.*" What does that mean?	**outlet**
6. What is one thing that you plug into an electrical *outlet* at home?	**outlet**
7. Look at the front of a quarter. Does it show George Washington in *profile* or facing the viewer?	**profile**
8. Whose *profile* would you enjoy reading?	**profile**
9. Think of a good friend of yours. Do you *recall* how the two of you first met?	**recall**
10. What is one reason why a manufacturer might *recall* a toy car?	**recall**
11. What memory of this school year will you *retain* for years to come?	**retain**
12. Who is someone in the news who *retains* at least one bodyguard?	**retain**

Link It: Make Word-to-World Connections

Give It a Day

Directions: For a full day, watch for ways the vocabulary words relate to your world. Keep a notebook handy and jot down every idea you have that day. For instance, you may hear a news report about a toy *recall*, you may read the *profile* of a musician, or you may *retain* your affection for a friend despite a disagreement.

Report back to your class. Tell them how many examples you collected and read a few aloud. Tell whether you noticed examples for every word, or if a word didn't show up in your world that week. Some vocabulary words have more meanings than are included in the word list. If you used one of these additional meanings, be sure to point that out.

Master It: Use Words in Meaningful Ways

Tell Me About It

Directions: Choose one of the following topics. Gather information on the topic and tell your class about it in an oral report.

> Explain how a *foil* is used in fencing. Show a picture of a foil, if possible.

> Explain safety precautions to take when using electrical *outlets*.

> Write a *profile* of a remarkable person.

> Explain how to *recall* key information for a test. Give tips for various subject areas.

> Explain how to *retain* your competitive edge between sports seasons.

> Get approval to write about a topic that you develop. Be sure that your topic uses a vocabulary word!

Vocabulary Mini-Lesson: Understanding Literal and Figurative Uses of Words

Most of the time, we use words according to their **literal** meaning, or dictionary definition. However, we can also use words **figuratively**. When you read figurative language, you must *interpret* the meaning instead of just defining the words. With figurative language, a writer creates a striking mental image or makes an idea memorable. Look at these examples.

Literal: This car weighs nearly two <u>tons</u>.

(The car literally weighs nearly two tons, about 4,000 pounds.)

Figurative: Our history teacher gave us <u>tons</u> of homework tonight.

(The teacher did not actually assign thousands of pounds of homework. It just seems that way, because there's so much to do.)

As you can see, when you use a word literally, you mean exactly what you say. When you use a word figuratively, you are expressing an idea creatively, not factually.

Here is another example of literal and figurative uses of a word.

Literal: With temperatures below zero, the lake was soon <u>frozen</u>.

(The water in the lake actually turned to ice.)

Figurative: I wish I had worn a warmer coat. I'm <u>frozen</u>!

(The speaker is very cold but did not actually turn to ice.)

When you read sentences that use words figuratively, remember this: The writer is expressing an idea creatively. You must interpret the figurative language in order to understand the word's use in the sentence. The table below will help you recognize ways words are used figuratively.

Type of Figurative Language	Explanation	Example
metaphor	a comparison of two things that says one thing *is* the other thing	The park was a <u>swamp</u> after the heavy rain.
simile	a comparison that uses a word such as *like* or *as*	The girl is as graceful as a <u>dancer</u>.
hyperbole	exaggeration to create an effect or to make a point	There are a <u>billion</u> people waiting in line ahead of us.

continued

| personification | giving human qualities, such as thoughts or speech, to animals or nonliving things | The alarm clock <u>screamed</u> that it was time to get up. |
| irony | a statement of the opposite of what is meant | An orange tie and pink shirt—what a <u>gorgeous</u> combination! |

When you see words used figuratively, as in the examples you just read, ask, "What image is the writer creating with this word?" or "What point is the writer making with this word?" These questions will help you understand the figurative use of a word.

Words to Know: Vocabulary Lists and Activities

In this section, you'll study two lists of words that are commonly used literally and figuratively.

List 27   Words Used Literally and Figuratively

Read each word, what it means, and how it's used both literally and figuratively. Note the kind of figurative language in each example.

Word	What It Means	How It's Used
beacon *(n)* BEE-kuhn	a lighthouse or signal fire used as a guide	*Literal:* Seeing the *beacon*, the searchers found the stranded hiker. *Metaphor:* Paul's smile was a *beacon* across the roomful of strangers. (Paul is not actually a light; his smile attracts you to him like a signal.)

continued

hibernate *(v)* HI-ber-nayt	to spend the winter in an inactive state, as do certain animals	*Literal:* Many mammals and reptiles *hibernate* during the winter months. *Simile:* Lonye stays inside when the weather turns cold, *hibernating* like a bear in a cave. (Comparing Lonye's behavior to that of a hibernating bear suggests that Lonye hides from the world during the winter.)
petrified *(adj)* PE-truh-fide	turned into stone or a substance of stonelike hardness	*Literal:* The pieces of *petrified* wood on display at the museum had been preserved for millions of years. *Hyperbole:* Gary was *petrified* when he saw the snake slither across the path. (Gary didn't really turn to stone; he just froze out of fright)
mourn *(v)* mawrn	to feel or express sorrow for	*Literal:* Everyone in town *mourned* the death of kindly Mrs. Ebal. *Personification:* Gray autumn skies seemed to *mourn* the passing of summer. (The sky cannot actually express emotions.)
recreation *(n)* rek-ree-AY-shuhn	any form of play or amusement intended for relaxation or refreshment	*Literal:* Fishing is Dad's favorite form of *recreation*, but I prefer gardening. *Irony:* Mom had some delightful *recreation* planned for me, beginning with mopping the floor. (The speaker is using irony to point out that the activity is *not* "delightful recreation.")

Own It: Develop Your Word Understanding

Divide and Conquer

Directions: Work with a partner to complete the activity. Here's what to do:

1. Divide the ten sentences that follow between you.

2. Read each of your sentences and decide if the underlined word is used literally or figuratively. Write *L* or *F* next to the sentence to indicate your answer.

3. Share your results with your partner and explain your answers.

4. In a class discussion, talk about sentences that were challenging or confusing. Revise your answers as necessary.

_____ 1. Your love is a <u>beacon</u>, guiding me out of sadness.

_____ 2. You can see <u>petrified</u> redwood trees in the Petrified Forest in California.

_____ 3. During winter, the western diamondback rattlesnake <u>hibernates</u> in caves.

_____ 4. At the military camp, kids were treated to <u>recreation</u> including long marches, hundreds of push-ups, and kitchen duty.

_____ 5. The abandoned old house <u>mourned</u> the days when a family lived in it.

_____ 6. The campfire was a <u>beacon</u> that led me back to the campsite.

_____ 7. Taking pictures with my camera is my favorite form of <u>recreation</u>.

_____ 8. Because Kim is allergic to bee stings, she is <u>petrified</u> of bees.

_____ 9. When my sister's fiancé broke up with her, she <u>mourned</u> for months.

_____ 10. After a bad haircut, Emilia said she was going to <u>hibernate</u> indoors forever.

Link It: Make Word-to-World Connections

Figurative Trading Cards

Directions: In this activity, you'll use vocabulary words figuratively to create trading cards. Here's what to do:

1. Gather supplies. You need five index cards, pens, paints, photos, and any other art supplies you want to use.

2. On each card, print one vocabulary word.

3. Draw or glue an image that corresponds to a figurative use of the word. For instance, on the *beacon* card, you could paste a photo of your soccer cleats or a football. To interpret this card, you would say that the shoes (or ball) are a beacon, guiding you from boredom to happiness. Be sure to sign your name somewhere on each card!

4. In class, take part in a Figurative Trading Card Festival. Move around the room, showing your cards to others. You may need

to interpret some cards for some people. Trade your cards for other cards that capture your interest.

Master It: Use Words in Meaningful Ways

Literal or Figurative?

Directions: In this activity, you'll practice using words literally and figuratively. Follow these steps:

1. Write five sentences, each one using a different vocabulary word. Use some vocabulary words literally, and use others figuratively. These sentences may tell something about yourself, your neighborhood, or something else from your world. (Use the Figurative Trading Card activity, above, for inspiration.) Try to use at least two or three different types of figurative language.

2. Trade sentences with a classmate. Read each sentence, and decide whether the vocabulary word is used literally or figuratively. Write *L* or *F* above the word to show your opinion.

3. Share the results with your classmate and talk about any sentences that were challenging.

List 28   Words Used Literally and Figuratively

Here are five additional words. Read each word, what it means, and how it's used both literally and figuratively. Note the kind of figurative language in each example.

Word	What It Means	How It's Used
unravel *(v)* uhn-RA-vuhl	to come apart as a result of threads separating	*Literal:* The sleeve of my sweater is beginning to *unravel*. *Metaphor:* Scientists are working hard to *unravel* the mystery of this disease. (Solving "the mystery" is being compared to separating threads.)
agile *(adj)* AJ-uhl	able to move quickly and easily	*Literal:* Billy wondered if he was *agile* and strong enough to become a dancer. *Simile: Agile* as a cat, the girl climbed up and over the fence. (Comparing the girl's movements to those of a cat is a vivid way of suggesting just how fast and graceful the girl is.)

continued

eternity *(n)* i-TUR-ni-TEE	time without end	*Literal:* Some people believe in an afterlife that is an *eternity* filled with joy. *Hyperbole:* It took me an *eternity* to write this ten-page essay. (I didn't really take forever to write the report; it just felt that way.)
summon *(v)* SUHM-uhn	to order to come; call for	*Literal:* The king *summoned* the knights to the palace. *Personification:* My warm blankets and soft pillow *summoned* me to bed. (Blankets and pillows cannot actually order someone to bed.)
diverse *(adj)* di-VURSE	varied; different	*Literal:* Maria has such *diverse* interests as gardening and woodworking. *Irony:* The snack bar gives you a choice of either fried, greasy foods or greasy, fried foods—what a *diverse* menu!

Own It: Develop Your Word Understanding

Two Sides of the Coin

Directions: Each vocabulary word is like a coin with two sides—a literal side and a figurative side. You have one coin, but more than one way to "spend" it. To become familiar with literal and figurative uses of each word, complete the graphic organizers. Follow these steps:

1. On the **Literal** side of the coin, write a sentence that uses the word literally. For example, *The agile goalie blocked the soccer ball.*

2. On the **Figurative** side of the coin, write a sentence that uses the word figuratively. For example, *The construction worker, agile as a dancer, walked along a high beam.*

3. In a class discussion, share some of your work.

Literal   Figurative

unravel

Literal   Figurative

agile

Literal   Figurative

eternity

Literal   Figurative

summon

Literal   Figurative

diverse

Link It: Make Word-to-World Connections

Spin the Bottle

Directions: In this activity, you'll practice using words literally and figuratively. First, your teacher will place you in small groups and give each group an empty plastic bottle. Then follow these steps:

1. Place the bottle on a desk in the center of your group. One of you spins the bottle. Wait for the bottle to stop, pointing at someone. Then ask this person, "Literal or figurative?" When the person chooses, give him or her a vocabulary word.

2. The person makes up a sentence that uses the vocabulary word literally or figuratively, depending on the choice made.

3. This person becomes the new bottle spinner, and the process repeats. If you run out of vocabulary words, use words from List 27 (pages 182–183).

Master It: Use Words in Meaningful Ways

Five-Minute Mastery

Directions: In this activity, you'll write very quickly for five minutes about *one* vocabulary word. Here's how the activity works:

1. Choose one vocabulary word for this activity.

2. Get out a sheet of paper and set a timer for five minutes. (Your teacher may watch the time for you.) Begin by writing the first thought in your head about the vocabulary word. This thought could be a definition, a sentence using the word, a memory inspired by the word, or any other thought. There is no "wrong" thing to write.

3. Keep writing. Don't stop! Use the word literally. Use it figuratively. Write questions, lines of poetry, descriptions, statements, phrases, and anything else that comes to mind. Let one thought lead into the next.

4. After five minutes, stop writing.

5. Read what you wrote. Indulge in feelings of satisfaction and pride in your five-minute mastery of the vocabulary word.

Vocabulary Mini-Lesson: Using Descriptive Words with Specific Meanings

As writers and speakers, we're always using words to describe people, places, and things. For example:

Mrs. Whitrock is a nice lady.

I read a good book last week.

Max is a big guy.

However, when you hear descriptions like these, the best you can do is guess at their meaning.

What makes Mrs. Whitrock a "nice" lady? Is she friendly? Helpful? Considerate?

What made it a "good" book? Was it exciting? Informative? Did it make you laugh?

In what sense is Max a "big" guy? Is he tall? Muscular? Overweight?

Describing words (adjectives) like *nice*, *good*, and *big* give only a general idea of meaning. They are not precise. By using specific descriptive words when you write and speak, you can convey your ideas more clearly. Like figurative language, descriptive words will help your reader or listener get a clear picture of what you mean.

Words to Know: Vocabulary Lists and Activities

In this section, you'll study two lists of words that are very specific and will help you describe people and events more clearly.

List 29   Words That Describe Physical Characteristics and Appearance

These ten words can be used to talk about what something looks, feels, or seems like. Notice how these words are specific and paint a very clear picture in your head. Read each word, what it means, and how it's used.

Word	What It Means	How It's Used
colossal *(adj)* kuh-LAH-suhl	huge; enormous; gigantic	The new skyscraper is *colossal*, more than fifty stories high.
comical *(adj)* KOM-i-kuhl	amusing; funny	Emma had a *comical* expression on her face when we all yelled, "Surprise!"
flimsy *(adj)* FLIM-zee	of poor quality; easily damaged	Our *flimsy* table cracked under the weight of the heavy television set.
fragile *(adj)* FRAH-juhl	easily broken	Please handle this glass statue with care because it's *fragile*.
frigid *(adj)* FRIH-jid	extremely cold	January weather in North Dakota is *frigid*, with temperatures well below zero.
hardy *(adj)* HAHR-dee	able to withstand difficult or unpleasant conditions	Despite the cold and rainy weather, the *hardy* adventurers camped overnight in the woods.

continued

primitive *(adj)* PRIHM-mi-tiv	not advanced; simple; crude	The villagers lived under *primitive* conditions, without electricity or indoor plumbing.
prominent *(adj)* PRAHM-muh-nuhnt	standing out; noticeable; conspicuous	Harry Potter has a *prominent* scar on his forehead.
treacherous *(adj)* TREH-cher-uhs	dangerous; hazardous	Hikers were advised to avoid the slippery rocks because the storm had made them *treacherous*.
turbulent *(adj)* TUR-byuh-luhnt	characterized by violent motion	As we traveled down the river, out raft was nearly overturned by the *turbulent* waters.

Own It: Develop Your Word Understanding

Box It

Directions: Fill in the boxes that surround each vocabulary word. List synonyms and antonyms of the key word, and list nouns that the key word could describe. Finally, sketch or write a memory cue to help you remember the word's meaning. (If your teacher approves, work with a partner to complete the activity.)

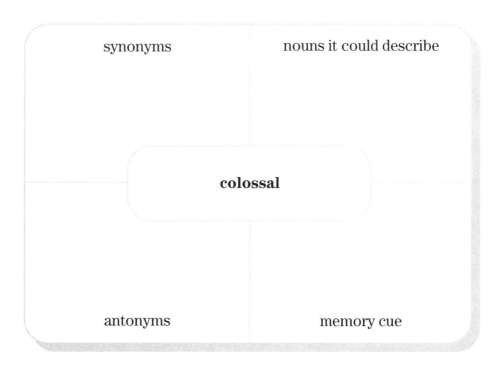

synonyms

nouns it could describe

colossal

antonyms

memory cue

synonyms   nouns it could describe

comical

antonyms   memory cue

synonyms   nouns it could describe

flimsy

antonyms   memory cue

synonyms   nouns it could describe

fragile

antonyms   memory cue

synonyms   nouns it could describe

frigid

antonyms   memory cue

synonyms   nouns it could describe

hardy

antonyms   memory cue

synonyms   nouns it could describe

primitive

antonyms   memory cue

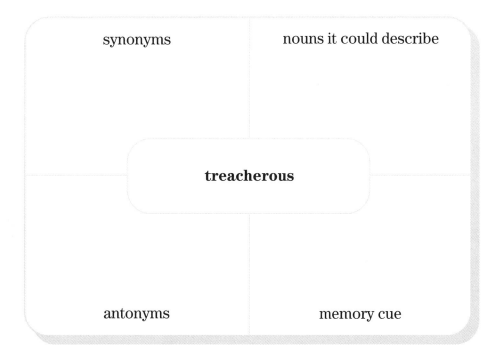

synonyms	nouns it could describe

turbulent

antonyms	memory cue

Link It: Make Word-to-World Connections

10 Things I Love About You

Directions: Pick a person (or a pet) and write sentences to describe things you love about him or her. Use all ten vocabulary words in your sentences—a task that requires you to get creative. For instance, *frigid* may not seem to have positive meaning, so how could you use it to describe something you love about someone?

One final note—when you write your list, you can change the person's name to protect your privacy!

Master It: Use Words in Meaningful Ways

Set Me Free—In Verse!

Directions: Free verse is a type of poetry that does not use a set rhyme or rhythm. Here is an example of free verse. Notice that the lines share a common theme, but there is no rhyme or meter.

Primitive Thoughts from the Heart

Your comical grin is infectious.

Your turbulence in sports is thrilling.

Your hardy spirit is inspiring.

You are colossal, larger-than-life—

My hero.

Create your own poem, written in free verse, using some of the vocabulary words. A fun way to start is to take phrases and sentences from your work in the 10 Things I Love About You activity. Edit and rearrange these phrases and sentences to form a poem. Then add the finishing touch: a title. Share your creation with classmates in a poetry festival.

List 30   Words That Describe Personality, Character, or Mood

These ten words can be used to describe a person or character. Notice how these kinds of words are much more specific than simply calling someone "good" or "bad," "nice" or "mean," "happy" or "sad." Read each word, what it means, and how it's used.

Word	What It Means	How It's Used
ambitious *(adj)* am-BISH-uhs	eager to achieve a particular goal	Elizabeth is an *ambitious* student who hopes to attend a top college.
brutal *(adj)* BROOT-l	cruel; harsh; merciless	The *brutal* dictator imprisoned people who opposed his views.
changeable *(adj)* CHAIN-juh-buhl	tending to change; variable	Matthew has a *changeable* nature, cheerful one day, gloomy the next.
fickle *(adj)* FIHK-kuhl	not constant or stable; not dependable; likely to change	*Fickle* friends are not around when you really need them.
hostile *(adj)* HOS-tl	having or showing ill will; unfriendly	The *hostile* crowd booed the unpopular speaker.
industrious *(adj)* in-DUHS-tree-uhs	hardworking	Ms. Finnegan gave Daniel a raise in pay because he is such an *industrious* worker.
jubilant *(adj)* JOO-buh-luhnt	in high spirits; joyful and triumphant	*Jubilant* fans celebrated their team's victory.
melancholy *(adj)* MEL-uhn-kol-ee	sad; gloomy; depressed	Reading about war leaves me in a *melancholy* mood.
sentimental *(adj)* sen-tuh-MEN-tl	having or showing tender feeling; influenced by emotion rather than reason	The singer sang a *sentimental* ballad about the first girl he had ever loved.
valiant *(adj)* VAL-yuhnt	brave; bold; courageous	The *valiant* soldiers marched into battle.

Own It: Develop Your Word Understanding

Accept or Reject?

Directions: In this activity, you'll spot fake definitions of the vocabulary words. Here's how the activity works:

1. Your teacher will assign you and a partner one of the vocabulary words. On an index card, write your names and the word you received. On the back of the card, write two things: a *correct* definition of the word, and an *incorrect* definition that you make up. (Label each definition.) Try to create incorrect definitions that are similar to the correct ones, so the activity is a bit more challenging.

2. Your teacher will mix everyone's cards together in a box.

3. Your teacher will pull out a card and read the vocabulary word aloud. Then he or she will read *one* of the definitions on the card. You must decide if the definition is correct or incorrect.

4. Your teacher will ask for a show of hands to indicate whether you *accept* or *reject* the definition. Be prepared to defend your vote!

Last week, I had a colossal pimple in a prominent position on my nose. I felt <u>melancholy</u> and thought Emily wouldn't want to go to the dance with me. It went away quickly, though, so now I feel <u>jubilant</u> and confident to ask her.

Link It: Make Word-to-World Connections

I'm Thinking of a Word . . .

Directions: In this activity, you and your classmates will use the vocabulary words to describe things in your own lives. Here's how the activity works:

1. Cut two strips of paper. On each one, write the name of something in your life that could be described by one of the vocabulary words. For instance, you might write *homework assignment* on one slip and *favorite song* on the other.

2. Your teacher will collect all the slips of paper and jumble them in a box. Then he or she will pull out one slip and read the word aloud.

3. Students suggest one or more vocabulary words that logically describe the word. (If the word is one of *your* two words, stay silent until others have had a chance to answer.)

4. Repeat the process with the next slip of paper pulled from the box.

Master It: Use Words in Meaningful Ways

Passion Club

Directions: What is your passion? Do you love motorcycles or skateboarding or singing? Maybe you are passionate about nature or fashion or softball. In this activity, you'll choose something that you're passionate about and plan a club based on this passion. Here's what to do:

1. Brainstorm a list of all the things you really like—things you're passionate about.

2. Choose one passion that some of your friends would enjoy sharing with you.

3. Plan a "passion club" based on this interest. To plan the club, think about some of these questions: What is the purpose of the club? Who can join? How often will the club meet? What will you do at club meetings? What is the club's name?

4. Create a flyer that announces your club and gives details about it. On the flyer, use some of the vocabulary words, or forms of the words.

5. You can hand out the flyer to your friends, or show it only to your teacher.

Wrapping Up: Review What You've Learned

Here's a brief summary of what you've studied in this chapter.

> Many words have more than one meaning. Familiar words often have less familiar additional meanings.

> When you use a word literally, you mean exactly what you say. When you use a word figuratively, you are expressing an idea creatively, not factually.

> Writers use figurative language to create a striking mental image or make an idea memorable. When you read figurative language, you must interpret the meaning instead of just defining the words. In this chapter, you looked at words that could be used in different types of figurative language

> > metaphor

> > simile

> > hyperbole

> > personification

> > irony

> Words such as *nice*, *good*, and *big* give only a general idea of meaning. They are not precise. Using specific descriptive words when you write and speak will help you express your ideas more clearly.

Flaunt It: Show Your Word Understanding

In the following exercises, you'll demonstrate your understanding of each vocabulary word. You will use vocabulary words, or forms of the words, to complete sentences and to write sentences of your own.

A Matching

Directions: Match the underlined word to its definition. Write the letter of the definition on the line provided.

_____ 1. The winter weather has been <u>brutal</u> this year.

_____ 2. Maine is known for the light-houses that stand as <u>beacons</u> on rocky cliffs.

_____ 3. Everything in Breanna's closet is either purple or black—what a <u>diverse</u> fashion sense!

_____ 4. The calm waters of this lake can quickly become <u>treacherous</u> in a storm.

_____ 5. I knew my lines for the play, but when the curtain rose I became <u>petrified</u>. I couldn't say a word.

_____ 6. Travis may be a teenager now, but he'll always <u>retain</u> his love of Saturday-morning cartoons.

_____ 7. Mariachi music is a traditional part of Mexican <u>culture</u>.

a. turned into stone or a substance of stonelike hardness

b. the customs, ideas, arts, and accomplishments of a nation or people

c. to continue to have or hold; to keep

d. any form of play or amusement intended for relaxation or refreshment

e. a light or signal used as a guide

f. cruel; harsh; merciless

g. brave; bold; courageous

h. time without end

i. dangerous; hazardous

j. varied; different

_____ 8. A <u>valiant</u> lifeguard dove into the choppy waves where the boater had fallen overboard.

_____ 9. My dad always says that sitting on the couch and watching football is a time-honored form of <u>recreation</u>.

_____ 10. Peace talks to end the war seemed to take an <u>eternity</u>.

B Sentence Completion

Directions: Circle the letter of the word that best completes each sentence.

11. The cactus is a _____ plant, for it can withstand high temperatures and little rainfall.

    a. frigid   **b.** hardy
    c. primitive   **d.** fragile

12. When it comes to movies, Jonas is _____. One week he likes comedies, and the next week he insists they are childish.

    a. industrious   **b.** sentimental
    c. jubilant   **d.** fickle

13. The sight of our new kitten standing on the dining room table, eating from a serving dish, was _____.

    a. agile   **b.** comical
    c. turbulent   **d.** colossal

14. When school ends for the year, I always feel _____ because I know I'll miss the friends and teachers that I had that year.

    a. jubilant   **b.** ambitious
    c. melancholy   **d.** flimsy

15. Eating fruits and vegetables is _____ with a healthy lifestyle.

    a. associated   **b.** summoned
    c. hostile   **d.** mourned

C Writing

Directions: On separate paper, write one or more sentences to answer each question. Be sure to use the vocabulary word.

16. What is one possible benefit to owning a *compact* car?

17. Would you ever change your *conviction* about something to please a friend?

18. Who are two people who serve as *foils* for one another?

19. What is your preferred *outlet* for excess energy?

20. Do you know someone whose *profile* looks similar to that of a parent?

21. Can you *recall* any events from being in kindergarten?

22. In which season of the year do some animals and reptiles *hibernate*?

23. What happy memory from the past year is most *prominent* in your mind?

24. In what way are you an *ambitious* person?

25. Do *changeable* fashions delight you, bore you, or frustrate you?

Activities à la Carte: Extend Your Word Knowledge

The activities on this page are presented à la carte, like items on a restaurant menu, meaning that you can choose from a variety of options. Your teacher may assign an activity or let you pick the one that tempts your appetite. If time allows, you might do more than one activity. All of the activities feature the same ingredient: **exploring the meanings of words**. Dig in!

Here I Am, World

Take a piece of writing or art that you created for this chapter (such as the poem in free verse or the figurative trading cards) and find an *outlet* for publication. For ideas, ask teachers or librarians about trustworthy publications or Web sites. For instance, *Teen Ink* publishes writing, art, and photos by teenagers. The Web site address is www.teenink.com.

Play Me a Tune

Get out the poem you wrote for the Set Me Free—In Verse! activity (page 196) and set it to music. Grab a few musicians, a lead singer, and—voila!—you've created a band with its first original song.

Compact = *Kompakt*

Do multiple-meaning words in this lesson have multiple meanings when translated into another language? Or must you translate the English word into several different words to get the range of meanings? Translate vocabulary words (and phrases using vocabulary words) into another language. Analyze the results and share your insights with the class.

You Take the Cake

Idioms are phrases that express a thought figuratively, not literally. That is, you can't understand the phrase by looking up the words in a dictionary. You have to learn what the phrase means within the culture that created it. Create an idiom poster to display in class. List a dozen or so idioms, and explain their meanings. Here are a few to get you started: go for broke, all thumbs, a slip of the tongue, in over your head.

But Wait! That's Not All

Some vocabulary words in this chapter have more meanings than those listed here. Often, these additional meanings are associated with different parts of speech. Identify some of these words and tell your class about additional meanings.

There, They're, or *Their*?

Homonyms are words that are spelled and pronounced the same but have different meanings, such as the multiple-meaning words in this chapter. **Homographs** are spelled alike but have different meanings, origins, and sometimes pronunciations. (Compare "Bandage the *wound*" and "I *wound* the string onto the spool.") And then there are **homophones**, which are pronounced the same but have different meanings, such as *hear* and *here*. To educate your classmates, create a three-column table that explains homonyms, homographs, and homophones, and give examples.

Song in My Heart

Song lyrics are a gold mine when it comes to figurative uses of words. Examine the lyrics of some of your favorite songs, looking for words used figuratively. How does this use of a word fire your imagination, touch your heart, or dazzle your mind's eye?

The One and Only—Or Not

Is English the only language that uses words figuratively? Find out and report back to your classmates. Give them examples from English and the other language to make your explanation clear.

On Second Thought

Pull out a piece of writing that you are working on for a class or other project. Pump up the word power in the piece by using descriptive words with clear meanings and by using words figuratively. Then pat yourself on the back for using tools of the trade.

Understanding Shades of Meaning

9

In Chapter 8, you learned about words with multiple meanings, figurative meanings, and descriptive meanings. In that chapter, you zoomed in to study words closely and precisely. In this chapter, you'll zoom out and study words from a broader view. You'll see how words carry shades of meaning, including positive and negative connotations, unspoken messages, and tone.

You can think of these shades of meaning as a word's ripple effects, like a stone dropped in a pond. When you use a word, you drop it into the pond of a conversation. It has meaning. But the word's life doesn't stop there. Your use of the word causes ripples, or shades of meaning, to move out and add dimension to the word.

As you'll see, a word's shades of meaning come just as much from our *use* of the words as they do from the word's definition.

Objectives

In this chapter, you will learn

> How a word can seem positive or negative
> How a word can be loaded with bias or attitudes
> How a word can carry an informal or formal tone

Sneak Peek: Preview the Lesson

Gut Reactions

In the following questions, some of the italicized words are vocabulary words in this chapter. Answer each question, giving your first response, or gut reaction. Don't worry about explaining *why* you answer the way you do. As you complete this lesson, you'll have opportunities to discuss why you might respond to a word in a particular way.

1. Would you rather be described as *assertive* or *pushy*?
   _____

2. Would you trust something known as *doublespeak*?
   _____

3. Which statement would be taken more seriously: saying that a problem is *significant*, or saying that it is a *freaking annoyance*? _____

4. With a friend, would you discuss how a movie *depicts* people, or how it *shows* them? _____

5. Would you expect a teacher to say, "Write a poem to *convey* an emotion" or "*Spit out* some emotional words in the form of a poem"? _____

Vocabulary Mini-Lesson: Words Have Feelings

Many words have meanings that are similar, but not exactly the same. Compare these sentences:

The chemical in the bottle had an unpleasant smell.

The chemical in the bottle had a disagreeable smell.

The chemical in the bottle had a horrible smell.

The chemical in the bottle had a sickening smell.

All five sentences describe the same chemical. Read the sentences again. What effect does changing a single word have on the image in your mind?

Here's another example:

Ethan ran up the stairs.

Ethan jogged up the stairs.

Ethan sprinted up the stairs.

Ethan scampered up the stairs.

Ethan raced up the stairs.

Again, changing one word changes your sense of the sentence. What was Ethan's mood when he ran up the stairs? Was he excited? Scared? Happy? You can't know for sure, because you don't know what's on his mind. However, a strong word *raced* suggests more urgency than milder words like *jogged* and *scampered*. Even though the words are similar in meaning, the feelings associated with them are different.

To talk about the feelings associated with words, it's helpful to understand two terms: denotation and connotation. The **denotation** of a word is its exact, literal meaning. For example, the denotation of *run* is "to go by rapidly moving the legs."

In addition to denotations, many (but not all) words have connotations. The **connotation** of a word is the impression the word makes in our mind. It's a feeling that is *suggested* but not stated. For example, look again at the following sentences:

The chemical in the bottle had a sickening smell.

Sickening has a different connotation from *unpleasant* or *disagreeable*. *Sickening* suggests that the chemical smell is much worse than just distasteful: it's bad enough to make you sick.

Ethan scampered up the stairs.

Scampered has an easygoing, almost playful connotation—less serious than *raced*, for example. Perhaps you think of squirrels scampering across a roof or children scampering around a playground. In other words, a writer wouldn't use a word like *scampered* if Ethan were running from extreme danger.

Look at these pairs of sentences.

Christopher is watchful. His friend is cautious.

Joshua is scrawny. His cousin is slender.

Olivia is daring. Her sister is reckless.

What is the denotation of the underlined words? Does each word also have a connotation? If so, do you think the connotation is generally positive or negative?

Words to Know: Vocabulary Lists and Activities

In this section, you'll study a list of words that have connotations. Read the example sentences carefully. Use the context to help you understand whether the word has a positive or negative connotation.

List 31 Words with Positive and Negative Connotations

Read each word, what it means, and how it's used. Think about the positive or negative meaning of each word.

Word	What It Means	How It's Used
assertive *(adj)* uh-SUR-tiv	confident and determined, as in expressing oneself	Ava is an *assertive* person who stands up for what she believes in.
brash *(adj)* brash	aggressive in an offensive way; impudent; pushy	That *brash* young man acts as though he's in charge, even though he's new to the team.
calculating *(adj)* KAL-kyuh-lay-ting	selfishly planning and scheming; deceitful	The *calculating* assistant was always trying to think of ways to impress his boss.
candid *(adj)* KAN-did	sincere; honest	I will ask Sophia for her opinion because she'll give me a *candid* answer.
falter *(v)* FAWL-ter	to show uncertainty; hesitate; waver	Abigail sounded strong at the start of the debate, but she *faltered* later on.
flexible *(adj)* FLEK-suh-buhl	able to change or adapt	I like to sleep late, but I can get up early when I need to; I'm *flexible*.
logical *(adj)* LAH-ji-kuhl	able to reason correctly; reasonable	Tony is a *logical* thinker who can solve any problem.
preoccupied *(adj)* pree-OK-yuh-pide	lost in thought	Emma was so *preoccupied* that she didn't get off the bus at her stop.
puny *(adj)* PYOO-nee	lacking in size, power, or importance; weak	The *puny* puppy needed special care to survive.
shrewd *(adj)* shrood	clever; sharp	The *shrewd* salesman knew just what to say to the customer to make the sale.

Own It: Develop Your Word Understanding

Connotations

Directions: In a small group, share your ideas about the connotation of each vocabulary word above. Follow these steps:

1. Start by having one person read a word aloud. Make sure everyone understands the word's meaning.

2. Then tell the group whether the word has mostly positive (pleasant) connotations or mostly negative (unpleasant) connotations to you. To help one another identify connotations, ask questions such as, "Would you want me to describe you as *puny*?" and "Would you rather be called *assertive* or *brash*?"

3. Based on the group discussion, complete the ten organizers
that follow. First, classify each word's connotation as positive
or negative. Then explain your answer by telling *why* you think
the word carries mainly pleasant or unpleasant overtones.

assertive

connotation

explanation of connotation

brash

connotation

explanation of connotation

calculating

connotation

explanation of connotation

candid

connotation

explanation of connotation

falter

connotation

explanation of connotation

flexible

connotation

explanation of connotation

logical

connotation

explanation of connotation

preoccupied

connotation

explanation of connotation

shrewd

connotation

explanation of connotation

puny

explanation of connotation

connotation

Link It: Make Word-to-World Connections

Welcome to My World

Directions: In this activity, you'll work alone and then with a group to link vocabulary words to your world. Here's what to do:

1. Play around with the vocabulary words, using them to make statements about yourself, friends, family members, your neighborhood, or other aspects of your life. Write at least five sentences using vocabulary words.

2. Choose three sentences that best describe your world. Cut your paper in strips, one sentence per strip.

3. In a small group, jumble everyone's sentences in a box. Take turns pulling out a sentence, reading it aloud, and guessing whose life it describes.

Master It: Use Words in Meaningful Ways

Popcorn and Movies

Directions: In this activity, you'll write a movie review to share with classmates. Follow these steps:

1. Choose a movie to review. It could be a movie that's out in theaters, a television movie, a home movie, a video rental—it's up to you. (If you are unable to watch a movie, talk to your teacher about reviewing a book instead.)

2. Watch the movie and takes notes as you do so. Keep the vocabulary words handy and jot down comments about the movie using these words.

3. Write your movie review. Tell readers what the movie is about (don't give away the ending!). Point out strong points and weak points of the movie and describe your favorite part.

4. With your teacher, plan a popcorn and movie event in class, when you'll snack on popcorn while people share their reviews. Afterward, you'll have enough movie recommendations to keep you entertained for a month!

Vocabulary Mini-Lesson: Words Contain Messages

Writers choose their words carefully. They know that the connotations of words shape readers' thoughts and opinions. Compare these two sentences:

> Because Mr. Broderick is such an intelligent man, many people believe in his concepts.

> Because Mr. Broderick is such a cunning man, many people believe in his schemes.

Which sentence do you think was written by an admirer of Mr. Broderick? How do you know?

Words like *intelligent* and *concepts* have positive connotations, while *cunning* and *schemes* have negative connotations. A writer can send an unspoken message to readers by choosing the words that express his or her own feelings. Unless you think about the connotations of words, you might not even realize a message is being sent!

Such unspoken messages are everywhere. They appear in newspaper and magazine articles, in TV commercials, and in printed advertisements. Be on the lookout for them. Think carefully about what you read and hear. Watch for words that are meant to win you over or persuade you to act or think in a certain way.

Words to Know: Vocabulary Lists and Activities

The words in List 32 relate to the sending of messages through written and spoken communication. You can use these words when you discuss articles and advertisements. These words will also help you think about the ways in which people try to persuade one another.

List 32   Words and Messages

Read each word, what it means, and how it's used.

Word	What It Means	How It's Used
analyze *(v)* A-nuh-lize	to break into parts in order to examine closely	If you *analyze* this advertisement, you'll find that the manufacturer includes few facts.
censor *(v)* SEN-ser	to examine and remove objectionable parts from	Some governments *censor* the news in order to hide information from the people.
convey *(v)* kuhn-VEY	to communicate; suggest	To *convey* positive images about their products, clothing commercials show happy, healthy-looking people.
depict *(v)* di-PIKT	to show; represent; portray	The artist's sketch *depicts* two well-dressed people entering a store.
doublespeak *(n)* DUH-buhl-speek	language meant to disguise or distort its true meaning; deceptive language	Not wanting to announce that it was firing employees, the company instead used *doublespeak* and said it was "downsizing."
evaluate *(v)* i-VAL-yoo-ate	to judge the significance, worth, or quality of	Researchers are *evaluating* the information they've gathered.
loaded *(adj)* LOH-did	using words with positive or negative connotations in order to affect people's feelings	Magazine advertisements use *loaded* language to influence readers.
objective *(adj)* uhb-JEK-tiv	without bias or prejudice, not affected by personal feelings (contrast *subjective*, below)	News reporters try to remain *objective* in their description of events.
persuasion *(n)* per-SWAY-zhuhn	ability to persuade; convincing through the use of argument	To win a trial, a lawyer must be skilled in the art of *persuasion*.
subjective *(adj)* suhb-JEK-tiv	affected by personal feelings, experience, or background (contrast *objective*, above)	The journalist wrote about the election from a *subjective* viewpoint.

Tip

To detect unspoken messages, pay close attention to the key words that writers and speakers choose to express their ideas. Keep in mind that nouns, verbs, adjectives, and adverbs can *all* have shades of meaning. Always consider both the denotation *and* the connotation of these words.

Own It: Develop Your Word Understanding

Word Pairs

Directions: The vocabulary words have been paired up in the following boxes. Each box also contains a few questions to help you think about the meanings of the words. With a partner, discuss and answer the questions in each box. Your teacher may ask you to share some of your ideas with the class.

---

analyze
evaluate

How are the meanings of these words alike?

Name something that you have *analyzed*.

Name something that you have *evaluated*.

---

censor
persuasion

Do you think school officials should

(a) *censor* materials in your school library? or

(b) *persuade* parents and teachers to discuss their concerns?

---

convey
depict

How are the meanings of these two words alike?

How do you *convey* a feeling of happiness?

How could you use words or images to *depict* a happy person?

**doublespeak
loaded**

How can *doublespeak* be used to soften the blow of bad news?

How can *loaded* words be used to soften the blow of bad news?

**objective
subjective**

How are the meanings of these two words different?

Would you rather have your friends evaluate you *objectively* or *subjectively*?

As you can tell, I am often preoccupied with Emily. I know I should <u>convey</u> my true feelings to her, but I'm afraid I would have to use lots of <u>persuasion</u> to get her to go out with me!

Link It: Make Word-to-World Connections

I'm Watching You

Directions: Put mass media under your microscope. For a week, take special notice of what you see, hear, and read in mass media. (Sources may include magazines, TV commercials, billboards, news stories, and more.) Share some of your observations and conclusions with the class. To frame your thoughts, you can choose to use some or all of these sentence starters:

Sentence Starters

> I *analyzed* a magazine advertisement for . . .

> I read a news story about *censorship* . . .

> This TV commercial *conveys* the idea that . . .

> Why do so many ads *depict* . . .

> An example of *doublespeak* that I found is . . .

> A product that I *evaluated* is . . .

> I spotted some *loaded* words in . . .

> A great place to look for *objective* articles is . . .

> I had to laugh at this effort at *persuasion* . . .

> I agree with this *subjective* report . . .

Master It: Use Words in Meaningful Ways

Ad Campaign

Directions: Imagine that you work for an advertising agency. You must develop an ad campaign for a client's product, and you must present your ideas in a meeting. To prepare for the meeting, follow these steps:

1. Divide a poster board down the center. On one half, create an advertisement for a product of your choosing (shoes, a music CD, food, or the like). On the other half, explain why the advertisement will be *effective* (why it will work).

2. Use art supplies, magazine cutouts, and other materials to create an ad for the product.

3. List five reasons why the ad will be effective. Use at least three of the vocabulary words to help express these reasons.

4. Present your poster and ideas in a small group or to the whole class, as directed by your teacher.

Vocabulary Mini-Lesson: Words Carry Tone

When was the last time you wore your fanciest clothes? Perhaps you attended a wedding or a special religious ceremony. No doubt, you selected your clothes with care. You didn't just pull on a sweatshirt and an old pair of jeans. You dressed in a way that was appropriate for the occasion.

Language is not so different from clothing. Writers and speakers choose words that are appropriate for the occasion. For instance, suppose you are writing an essay for English about a novel that you enjoyed reading. You might describe the book as "fascinating" or "absorbing." If you were talking to another student, though, you might simply say the book was "cool."

Just as you wouldn't wear jeans to a wedding, you wouldn't use slang for a school essay. Similarly, writers don't use chatty, casual language when they create serious documents, such as reports or business letters. Instead, they choose more formal language. Such language may not always be the simplest way to express ideas. However, it does add "weight" to what is being said. Formal words send an unspoken message: *This is a serious matter.*

Words to Know: Vocabulary Lists and Activities

The words in List 33 can be used in all sorts of formal situations, such as in an essay for school, a job application, a letter to a person of authority, or a company report. What other formal situations can you think of?

List 33   Formal Words

Read each word, what it means, and how it's used.

Word	What It Means	How It's Used
assurance *(n)* uh-SHOOHR-uhns	a pledge or promise; guarantee	Please give me your *assurance* that this package will be delivered on time.
circulate *(v)* SUR-kyuh-layt	to send around from person to person or place to place	Students *circulated* a petition requesting more food choices for the cafeteria menu.

continued

confidential *(adj)* kon-fi-DEN-shuhl	private; secret	The information in this envelope is *confidential*, so you may not show it to anyone else.
effective *(adj)* i-FEK-tiv	producing a desired effect or result	This medicine is an *effective* treatment for an upset stomach.
fundamental *(adj)* fuhn-duh-MEN-tl	basic; essential; underlying	Equality is a *fundamental* principle of democracy.
influential *(adj)* in-floo-EN-shuhl	able to exert influence on others; powerful; important	Mr. Smithers is the most *influential* member of the committee; everyone listens to him.
objective *(n)* uhb-JEK-tiv	a goal or aim	The army's immediate *objective* is to take control of the town.
satisfactory *(adj)* sat-is-FAK-tuh-ree	able to fulfill a need, requirement, or demand; acceptable	Jamil's story that someone else ate the cookies was not *satisfactory*; he had chocolate on his hands and crumbs on his shirt.
significant *(adj)* sig-NIH-fi-kuhnt	worthy of note; important	Medical researchers have made *significant* progress in their search for a cure.
warrant *(v)* WAWR-uhnt	to serve as reason for; justify; call for	These odd events *warrant* further investigation.

Own It: Develop Your Word Understanding

Eeny Meeny Miney Moe

Directions: Choosing the right word for the occasion is a sign of a well-educated person. In this activity, you'll explore a range of words and expressions that can mix and match with the vocabulary words. Work with a partner to complete the activity.

Each vocabulary word is listed in the Formal column. In the Informal column, write one or more informal synonyms. Two samples are provided to get you started.

Formal Word	Informal Synonym(s)
assurance	*promise*

continued

circulate	*pass around*
confidential	
effective	
fundamental	
influential	
objective	
satisfactory	
significant	
warrant	

Link It: Make Word-to-World Connections

In Other Words

Directions: In this activity, you'll practice expressing one thought in two ways: formally and informally. Pair up with a different person than your partner for the activity above. With your new partner, follow these steps:

1. Talk about when you have used the vocabulary words or the related informal synonyms, idioms, or slang. Help each other understand any words whose meanings are still unclear.

2. In the list of vocabulary words (pages 217–218), look at the third column, How It's Used. Your task is to rewrite each example sentence using an informal synonym or idiom instead of the formal vocabulary word.

3. Read some of your new sentences aloud to the class.

Master It: Use Words in Meaningful Ways

In All Seriousness

Directions: Rules govern our lives at school, work, and play, no matter our age. Some rules are fair and necessary; others may be unfair or unnecessary. Think of a rule that you must follow that seems unfair or unnecessary to you. Write a formal letter to the person who enforces this rule, explaining why you think the rule is not needed. In your letter, use at least four vocabulary words (or forms of them).

Give a copy of your letter to your teacher. It's up to you whether to deliver a copy of the letter to its addressee.

Wrapping Up: Review What You've Learned

Here's a brief summary of what you've studied in this chapter.

> Many words have meanings that are similar but not exactly the same. Often when two words have similar meanings, one of the words seems to have a negative feeling while the other leaves a more positive impression.

> The **denotation** of a word is its exact, literal meaning. Many words also have connotations. The **connotation** of a word is the impression the word makes in our mind. It is a feeling that is suggested but not stated.

> By choosing a word with a positive or negative connotation, the writer can change the reader's understanding of the sentence.

> Writers choose their words carefully because they know that the connotations of words shape readers' thoughts and opinions. A writer can send an unspoken message—positive or negative—by choosing words that express his or her own feelings.

> Unspoken messages appear in both written and spoken communication, such as newspaper and magazine articles, TV commercials, and printed advertisements. Such messages are meant to persuade people to act or think in a certain way.

> Writers and speakers choose words that are appropriate for the occasion. When serious language is called for, they don't use chatty, casual language. Instead, they use more formal language that adds "weight" to what is being said.

Flaunt It: Show Your Word Understanding

In the following exercises, you'll demonstrate your understanding of each vocabulary word. You will use vocabulary words, or forms of the words, to complete sentences and to write sentences of your own.

 A Word Bank

Directions: Choose a word from the box to complete each sentence. Write the word on the line provided. Each word may be used only once.

> candid   convey   objective   assurance   significant
> evaluates   shrewd   calculating   subjective   flexible

1. When the police questioned Rocky, his answers were _____ and suggested innocence of the crime. As a result, the officers let him go free.

2. My mother is a/an _____ shopper. She doesn't buy a lot of extra things just because they are on sale.

3. A sense of humor is one of the most _____ things that I look for in a friend.

4. It is difficult to be _____ when judging a family member. This is why parents are not allowed on the judging committee of the talent show.

5. Please give me your _____ that you accept my apology and won't stay angry with me.

6. We need volunteers who are _____. For instance, we may need them to work during the morning on Monday and in the afternoon on Wednesday.

7. When Mr. Bleau _____ an essay, he looks at the grammar as well as the organization and the ideas.

8. The _____ employee watched for an opportunity to cause her coworker to make a mistake so that she herself could step in and "save the day."

9. Beauty is _____. That is why some people seem to become more attractive the longer you know them.

10. This bouquet of flowers is to meant to _____ my gratitude to you.

B Sentence Completion

Directions: Circle the letter of the word that best completes each sentence.

11. Anything that you discuss with the school counselor is _____. This information will not be shared with your parents except in case of danger to yourself or others.
    - **a.** influential
    - **b.** assertive
    - **c.** confidential
    - **d.** doublespeak

12. All week, Rhonda has seemed _____. I wonder if she is going through a difficult time?
    - **a.** preoccupied
    - **b.** logical
    - **c.** satisfactory
    - **d.** effective

13. Tanner decided to _____ a photo of his stolen bicycle in hopes that someone had seen who took it.
    - **a.** analyze
    - **b.** circulate
    - **c.** warrant
    - **d.** censor

14. The apples from this year's crop seem _____ in comparison to those of last year's crop.
    - **a.** puny
    - **b.** brash
    - **c.** fundamental
    - **d.** loaded

15. Ms. Smith said, "You can use words or images to _____ your idea of what King Henry VIII looked like."
    - **a.** depict
    - **b.** persuade
    - **c.** warrant
    - **d.** falter

C Writing

Directions: Follow the directions to write sentences using vocabulary words. Write your sentences on a separate sheet of paper.

16. Use *objective* to express a goal or aim that you have.

17. Use *logical* in a sentence about a teacher.

18. Use *falter* in a sentence about a friend.

19. Use *censor* in a sentence that expresses an opinion.

20. Use *effective* to ask a question.

Chapter Extension Activities

Activities à la Carte: Extend Your Word Knowledge

The activities on this page are presented à la carte, like items on a restaurant menu, meaning that you can choose from a variety of options. Your teacher may assign an activity or let you pick the one that tempts your appetite. If time allows, you might do more than one activity. All of the activities feature the same ingredient: **shades of meaning in words**. Dig in!

Let's Disagree

Using vocabulary words as inspiration, write a few controversial statements—that is, statements about which people are likely to disagree. An example is *Censorship is necessary.* Then plan and carry out a five-minute debate based on one of these statements. Your classmates, as your audience, may vote to indicate who wins the debate.

I Have a Dream

With vocabulary words in mind, examine a famous or inspirational speech. Does the speaker use formal or informal language? Is the speech *objective* or *subjective*? Does the speaker use *loaded* words? Does the speaker seem *candid* or *calculating*? Point out parts of the speech that help you answer these and other questions. Report back to your class, or get permission to give an oral report in a related class, such as history.

Wordplay

Some people invent secret codes, and others learn the slang of new friends. Some people buy boxes of magnetic words and arrange them into poems on the refrigerator. Why? People like to play with the shades of meaning in words. Choose an art form and play with some words of your choosing. You might make a collage of words ripped from newspaper headlines, for example, or print words from this chapter and adorn them with images that they inspire. Display your wordplay in your classroom.

Environmental Print

For a week, keep an observation notebook about environmental print. This is the writing that you see on signs, notices, billboards, banners, and other printed matter in public places. Which examples use formal language? Which use informal language? Do any signs use words with strong negative or positive connotations, or are the words neutral? Do you see loaded words? Doublespeak? Share your findings with your class.

ELL What Did You Just Say?

A professional translator must master not only the vocabulary of a second language but also connotations of words in that language. Find out about the career path of translation and report back to your class. What kinds of jobs can a translator get? Why is connotation so important to the job of translation?

Devil's Advocate

Find an advertisement or argument that seems convincing. Then play devil's advocate by making a case for the opposite point of view. For instance, look for *doublespeak* that puts a positive spin on a quality that may be negative. A maker of sugary breakfast cereal, for instance, may reduce the grams of sugar per serving by one gram, then claim the cereal is "Now Healthier!" Could you argue that the change does not *warrant* this claim?

Word Doctor

Pull out a paper or project that you are writing for a class. Edit your word choices by replacing informal and slang words with formal words and expressions. In addition, *analyze* your use of adjectives and verbs. Could you replace mediocre, vague words with vivid, precise ones? (See the mini-lesson on the feeling of words, on page 206.)

Encore! Encore!

In this book, you've studied scores of vocabulary words. Which words confounded you? Delighted you? Inspired you? Choose 52 words and use them to create a Word of the Week calendar. You can recycle an old calendar by pasting new paper on it, use scrap paper and a hole punch, or design and print out pages. For each word, give a pronunciation guide, a definition, and an example sentence.

Using a Dictionary

A dictionary entry usually gives you the following information about a word:

> The pronunciation and how it's divided into syllables. The pronunciation is either given as a respelling, which shows you how to sound out the word (as done in this book), or it is given using what's called diacritical marks, or symbols. (Dictionaries with diacritical marks have keys that show you what those marks mean.) Hyphens or spaces are used to show how a word is divided into syllables.

> The part of speech

> The different definitions, sometimes with sample phrases or definitions

> Other forms of the word and their parts of speech

> Synonyms

as•so•ci•ate (uh-SOH-shee-ayt)

Etymology: from the Latin *ad* + *sociare*, to join

Date: 14th century

associate *(v)* **1** to join as partner or friend **2** to join or connect together; combine

Synonym: see *join*

associate (uh-SOH-shee-it) *(n)* **1** someone associated with another; partner; companion **2** employee; worker

Appendix B

Dictionary Sources

Following is a list of some of the many dictionary sources available to you.

Free Online Dictionaries

> **Merriam-Webster Online.** www.m-w.com. This site contains a dictionary, a thesaurus, a Spanish/English dictionary, and audio pronunciations.

> **Dictionary.com**. www.dictionary.com. Here, you can find a dictionary, a thesaurus, audio pronunciations, a reference tool, and a translation tool with over 30 languages.

> **Yourdictionary.com**. www.yourdictionary.com. This site's features include audio pronunciations, synonyms, and usage examples.

Dictionary Subscriptions

> **Oxford English Dictionary**. www.oed.com. Available by paid subscription online, or on CD-Rom.

> **Merriam-Webster Unabridged Dictionary**. www.m-w.com. This online dictionary, available by paid subscription, contains more definitions than Merriam-Webster's free online dictionary.

Print Dictionaries

Check your local bookstore or an online store like Amazon to see all the different kinds of dictionaries available to you. Here are two of the most basic and widely-used dictionaries.

> *The Merriam-Webster English Dictionary.* (For a more concise dictionary, check out *Merriam-Webster's Pocket Dictionary* or *Merriam-Webster's Collegiate Dictionary*, and more)

> *Concise Oxford English Dictionary*

A

abrupt (uh-BRUHPT) *(adj)*: sudden; unexpected

abruptness (uh-BRUHPT-ness) *(n)*: suddenness; unexpectedness

absorbent (ab-SAWR-buhnt) *(adj)*: able to absorb or soak up

access (AK-ses) *(n)*: the right or ability to approach, enter, or use

accuracy (AK-yer-uh-see) *(n)*: quality of being accurate; correctness

Achilles' heel (uh-KIL-eez heel) *(n)*: a vulnerable point; weak spot

acute (uh-KYOOT) *(adj)*: sharp and severe

adrenaline (uh-DREN-l-in) *(n)*: a hormone that is released in response to stress, to help you get through it

afterlife (AF-ter-lahyf) *(n)*: existence after death

agile (AJ-uhl) *(adj)*: able to move quickly and easily

algebra (AL-juh-bruh) *(n)*: a branch of mathematics

alibi (AL-uh-bie) *(n)*: the claim or fact that a person was in a different place when a crime was committed and so could not have committed the crime

alleviate (uh-LEE-vee-ate) *(v)*: to lessen or relieve

ambitious (am-BISH-uhs) *(adj)*: eager to achieve a particular goal

analyze (A-nuh-lize) *(v)*: to break into parts in order to examine closely

ancestry (AN-ses-tree) *(n)*: line of descent; family descent; ancestors

angelic (an-JEH-lik) *(adj)*: like or having the qualities of an angel

anticipate (an-TIS-uh-payt) *(v)*: to look forward to; expect

appendage (uh-PEN-dij) *(n)*: an attached part of an animal or plant

appendix (uh-PEN-diks) *(n)*: additional material at the end of a book or other written document

appreciative (uh-PREE-shuh-tiv) *(adj)*: feeling or showing appreciation; grateful

apprehension (ap-ri-HEN-shun) *(n)*: the condition of being anxious or fearful of something

aquatic (uh-KWA-tik) *(adj)*: occurring in or on water; relating to water

artisan (AHR-tuh-zuhn) *(n)*: a worker skilled in a trade or craft; craftsperson

assertive (uh-SUR-tiv) *(adj)*: confident and determined, as in expressing oneself

associate (uh-SOH-shee-ayt) *(v)*: to connect in one's mind; to spend time (with); join as a companion

assurance (uh-SHOOHR-uhns) *(n)*: a pledge or promise; guarantee

asterisk (AS-tuh-risk) *(n)*: a star-shaped mark (*) that is used in printing or writing to indicate a footnote

astronomy (uh-STRON-uh-mee) *(n)*: the scientific study of the stars, planets, and other objects in the universe

atlas (AT-luhs) *(n)*: a book of maps

attractiveness (uh-TRAK-tiv-ness) *(n)*: the quality of being attractive; pleasant appearance

avatar (AV-uh-tahr) *(n)*: an electronic image that represents a person on the computer (usually during a game)

avert (uh-VURT) *(v)*: to turn away; avoid

B

beacon (BEE-kuhn) *(n)*: a lighthouse or signal fire used as a guide

beautify (BYOO-tuh-fie) *(v)*: to make beautiful

befriend (bi-FREND) *(v)*: to act as a friend to

belittle (bi-LIT-l) *(v)*: to cause to seem less important; treat as unimportant

biographical (bie-uh-GRAF-i-kuhl) *(adj)*: relating to a person's life

biography (bie-OG-ruh-fee) *(n)*: a written account of a person's life

biological (bahy-uh-LOJ-i-kuhl) *(adj)*: relating to biology, the scientific study of plant and animal life

bling or **bling-bling** (bling) *(n)*: flashy or expensive jewelry or other possessions

blood pressure (bluhd PRESH-er) *(n)*: the pressure of the blood against the walls of the blood vessels, especially the arteries

blowhole (BLO-hohl) *(n)*: a nostril in the top of the head of certain sea mammals

boomerang (BOO-muh-rang) *(n)*: a flat, curved piece of wood, used as a weapon, that can be thrown so that it will return to the thrower

braille (breyl) *(n)*: a system of writing and printing for blind people that uses characters made up of raised dots, which are read through finger touch

brash (brash) *(adj)*: aggressive in an offensive way; impudent; pushy

breach (breech) *(v)*: to leap out of the water

brigade (bri-GAYD) *(n)*: a large military unit

broaden (BRAWD-n) *(v)*: to make wider; expand

browser (BROU-zer) *(n)*: computer software used to access Internet Web sites

brutal (BROOT-l) *(adj)*: cruel; harsh; merciless

burial (BER-ee-uhl) *(adj)*: relating to the burying of a dead body

C

calculating (KAL-kyuh-lay-ting) *(adj)*: selfishly planning and scheming; deceitful

candid (KAN-did) *(adj)*: sincere; honest

carjacking (KAHR-jak-ing) *(n)*: (blend of *car* and *hijacking*) the forcible taking of an automobile from its driver

carnivore (KAHR-nuh-vawr) *(n)*: a flesh-eating mammal

cavalry (KAV-uhl-ree) *(n)*: originally, a military unit that fought on horseback, but now may use motorized vehicles

censor (SEN-ser) *(v)*: to examine and remove objectionable parts from

changeable (CHAIN-juh-buhl) *(adj)*: tending to change; variable

circulate (SUR-kyuh-layt) *(v)*: to send around from person to person or place to place

clamorous (KLAM-er-uhs) *(adj)*: loud and noisy

clarify (KLAR-uh-fie) *(v)*: to make clear; explain

clone (klohn) *(v)*: to make a copy of

clumsiness (KLUHM-zee-nis) *(n)*: quality of being clumsy

colossal (kuh-LAH-suhl) *(adj)*: huge; enormous; gigantic

comical (KOM-i-kuhl) *(adj)*: amusing; funny

compact (KOM-pakt) *(adj)*: closely and firmly packed together; solid; arranged within a small space; occupying little space; brief and to the point; concise

compete (kump-PEET) *(v)*: to try to win or gain something that others want; be in rivalry with

competitive (kuhm-PEH-ti-tiv) *(adj)*: involving or based on the efforts of people who are competing

compromise (KOM-pruh-mize) *(n)*: settlement of a difference of opinion through agreement by both sides

compromise (KOM-pruh-mize) *(v)*: means of agreement; settlement

computerize (kuhm-PYOO-tuh-rize) *(v)*: to operate or control by means of computers

confer (kuhn-FUR) *(v)*: to consult together and compare views and opinions

confetti (kuhn-FEHT-tee) *(n)*: small pieces of colored paper made for throwing at celebrations

confidential (kon-fi-DEN-shuhl) *(adj)*: private; secret

conscientious (kon-shee-EN-shuhs) *(adj)*: very careful and exact

consciousness (KON-shuhs-nis) *(n)*: condition of being conscious

conspiracy (kuhn-SPIR-uh-see) *(n)*: a secret joining together in order to plan and carry out an unlawful or harmful act; plot

contradiction (kon-truh-DIK-shuhn) *(n)*: a statement that conflicts with itself; inconsistent statement; a denial

convenient (kuhn-VEEN-yuhnt) *(adj)*: easy to do or use; suitable

convey (kuhn-VEY) *(v)*: to communicate; suggest

convict (kuhn-VIKT) *(v)*: to judge or prove to be guilty of a crime

conviction (kuhn-VIK-shuhn) *(n)*: act or result of proving (a person) guilty of a crime; strong belief

cookie (KOOK-ee) *(n)*: a small file or part of a file stored on a computer, containing information about the user

copyright (KOP-ee-rite) *(n)*: the exclusive right to reproduce, publish, or sell an original work

croissant (kruh-SAHNT) *(n)*: a flaky roll shaped like a crescent

culture (KUHL-cher) *(n)*: the customs, ideas, arts, and accomplishments of a nation or people; refined and educated ways of thinking, speaking, and behaving

cybercafe (SY-ber-ka-FAY) *(n)*: a coffee shop that provides computers for customers to access the Internet

czar (zahr) *(n)*: formerly, an emperor of Russia

D

database (DEY-tuh-beys) *(n)*: a large collection of data organized for rapid search by a computer user

debris (duh-BREE) *(n)*: the remains of something that has been broken or destroyed

debut (day-BYOO) *(n)*: first public appearance

decibel (DES-uh-bel) *(n)*: unit for measuring the loudness of sound (one-tenth of a bel)

defiant (di-FIE-uhnt) *(adj)*: openly resisting; bold

deficient (dih-FIH-shunt) *(adj)*: missing a necessary substance, quality, or element

demolish (di-MOL-ish) *(v)*: to tear down; destroy

dependent (di-PEN-duhnt) *(adj)*: relying on another for support or care

depict (di-PIKT) *(v)*: to show; represent; portray

descriptive (di-SKRIP-tiv) *(adj)*: that describes

descriptively (di-SKRIP-tiv-lee) *(adv)*: in a way that describes

despise (di-SPIZE) *(v)*: to regard with strong negative feeling; scorn

diagnosis (die-uhg-NOH-sis) *(n)*: identification of a disease by studying its signs and symptoms

digest (di-JEST) *(v)*: to change (food) into a form that the body can absorb; to think over so as to fully understand

disability (dis-uh-BIHL-ih-tee) *(n)*: a condition that may reduce or interfere with certain physical or mental activities

disable (dis-AY-buhl) *(v)*: to make unable to act or operate

disaster (di-ZAS-ter) *(n)*: an event that causes great harm or damage

discontentedly (dis-kuhn-TEN-tid-lee) *(adv)*: in a way that shows displeasure or unhappiness

dishonestly (dis-ON-ist-lee) *(adv)*: in a way that's not truthful

dislocate (DIS-loh-kayt) *(v)*: to put out of place, especially to move a bone from normal connection to another bone

disrespect (dis-ri-SPEKT) *(n)*: lack of respect

distrust (dis-TRUHST) *(v)*: to have no trust or confidence in

disunity (dis-YOO-ni-tee) *(n)*: the condition of not being united; disagreement

diverse (di-VURSE) *(adj)*: varied; different

dorsal (DAWR-suhl) *(adj)*: near or on the back

doublespeak (DUH-buhl-speek) *(n)*: language meant to disguise or distort its true meaning; deceptive language

dramatically (druh-MA-tih-kalee) *(adv)*: in a dramatic or striking way

E

echolocation (ek-oh-loh-KAY-shuhn) *(n)*: the process of determining the position of objects by sending out sound waves, which are reflected back to the sender as echoes

ecology (i-KOL-uh-jee) *(n)*: the scientific study of the relation between living things and their environment

effective (i-FEK-tiv) *(adj)*: producing a desired effect or result

emission (i-MISH-uhn) *(n)*: something emitted or sent out

enact (en-AKT) *(v)*: to establish by legal authority (in particular: to make a bill into law)

enforce (en-FAWRS) *(v)*: to carry out or cause to do forcibly

envision (en-VIH-zhuhn) *(v)*: to picture in the mind; imagine

eternity (i-TUR-ni-tee) *(n)*: time without end

etiquette (ET-i-ket) *(n)*: the behavior and manners considered acceptable or required in social situations

evaluate (i-VAL-yoo-ate) *(v)*: to judge the significance, worth, or quality of

evident (EV-i-duhnt) *(adj)*: easy to see; clear; plain

exceed (ik-SEED) *(v)*: to go beyond

excessively (ik-SES-iv-lee) *(adv)*: beyond what would be expected; extremely

F

facilitate (fuh-SIH-li-tayt) *(v)*: to make easy or easier

falter (FAWL-ter) *(v)*: to show uncertainty; hesitate; waver

familiarize (fuh-MIL-yuh-rize) *(v)*: to make familiar or acquainted

fauna (FAW-nuh) *(n)*: the animals of a region, time period, or other group

fiancé (male)**, fiancée** (female) (fee-ahn-SAY) *(n)*: a man or woman engaged to be married

fickle (FIHK-kuhl) *(adj)*: not constant or stable; not dependable; likely to change

fictional (FIK-shuh-nuhl) *(adj)*: of fiction; imagined

flexible (FLEK-suh-buhl) *(adj)*: able to change or adapt

flimsy (FLIM-zee) *(adj)*: of poor quality; easily damaged

flora (FLOHR-uh) *(n)*: the plant life of a region, time period, or other group

foil (foil) *(n)*: a thin sheet of metal; a person or thing that sets off the qualities of another by contrast; a long, flexible fencing sword

forearm (FAWR-arm) *(n)*: the part of the arm between the elbow and the wrist

forecast (FAWR-kast) *(n)*: an estimate of what will happen; prediction

foresee (fawr-SEE) *(v)*: to see or know beforehand

fracture (FRAK-cher) *(n)*: the breaking of a body part

fragile (FRAH-juhl) *(adj)*: easily broken

fraud (frawd) *(n)*: intentional deception; trickery

frequency (FREE-kwuhn-see) *(n)*: fact of being frequent; occurring often

frigid (FRIH-jid) *(adj)*: extremely cold

frustration (fruh-STRAY-shuhn) *(n)*: a feeling of annoyance; irritation

fundamental (fuhn-duh-MEN-tl) *(adj)*: basic; essential; underlying

G

gadget (GAJ-it) *(n)*: an electronic or mechanical device

geographically (jee-uh-GRAF-i-kuhl-lee) *(adv)*: with regard to geography

GPS (gee-pee-ess) *(n)*: (short for *Global Positioning System*) a navigational system that uses satellite signals to track the user's position

grassroots (GRAS-roots) *(adj)*: starting or operating at the local level; involving ordinary citizens

groove (groov) *(n)*: a fixed routine

guardian (GAHR-dee-uhn) *(n)*: a person legally responsible for the care of another person

guillotine (GIL-uh-teen) *(n)*: a machine for beheading by means of a heavy blade dropped between two vertical posts

H

hacker (HAK-er) *(n)*: a person who illegally gains access to files in a computer system

hardy (HAHR-dee) *(adj)*: able to withstand difficult or unpleasant conditions

heighten (HIGH-tn) *(v)*: *to make* more intense; increase

hibernate (HI-ber-nayt) *(v)*: to spend the winter in an inactive state, as do certain animals

historically (hi-STAWR-ih-klee) *(adv)*: according to history

homeward (HOHM-werd) *(adv)*: toward home

hostile (HOS-tl) *(adj)*: having or showing ill will; unfriendly

hybrid (HIE-brid) *(adj)*: having two or more sources of power

I

illegal (i-LEE-guhl) *(adj)*: not legal; against the law

immortal (i-MAWR-tl) *(adj)*: living forever; everlasting

inclusive (in-KLOO-siv) *(adj)*: including everything; complete

independently (in-di-PEN-duhnt-lee) *(adv)*: on one's own; separately from others

indigestion (in-di-JES-chuhn) *(n)*: discomfort resulting from difficulty digesting food

industrious (in-DUHS-tree-uhs) *(adj)*: hardworking

influential (in-floo-EN-shuhl) *(adj)*: able to exert influence on others; powerful; important

influenza (in-floo-EN-zuh) *(n)*: a contagious disease caused by a virus

inhale (in-HAYL) *(v)*: to draw into the lungs; breathe in

inject (in-JEKT) *(v)*: to force into, as by using a hypodermic needle

innumerable (i-NOO-mer-uh-buhl) *(adj)*: too many to be counted

inscribe (in-SKRIBE) *(v)*: to write, mark, or engrave

insistent (in-SIS-tuhnt) *(adj)*: demanding attention; impossible to ignore

interact (in-ter-AKT) *(v)*: to act on or in relation with; deal with

intranet (IN-truh-net) *(n)*: a network that functions like the Internet, but where access is restricted to certain people (such as employees at a certain company)

J

jubilant (JOO-buh-luhnt) *(adj)*: in high spirits; joyful and triumphant

L

lawsuit (LAW-soot) *(n)*: a case before a court

lengthwise (LENGKTH-wahyz) *(adv)*: in the direction of the length

leotard (LEE-uh-tahrd) *(n)*: a close-fitting one-piece garment worn by dancers and acrobats

liberate (LIH-buh-rayt) *(v)*: to make or set free

likewise (LAHYK-wahyz) *(adv)*: in the same manner; similarly

loaded (LOH-did) *(adj)*: using words with positive or negative connotations in order to affect people's feelings

logical (LAH-ji-kuhl) *(adj)*: able to reason correctly; reasonable

loyalty (LOI-uhl-tee) *(n)*: fact of being loyal

lurk (lurk) *(v)*: to read messages on an Internet chat room or other group without contributing

M

marathon (MAR-uh-thuhn) *(n)*: a footrace of 26 miles, 385 yards

marriage (MAR-ij) *(n)*: condition of being married

matrilineal (mat-truh-LIN-ee-uhl) *(adj)*: tracing descent through the mother's family

maturity (muh-CHOOR-i-tee) *(n)*: quality of being mature

melancholy (MEL-uhn-kol-ee) *(adj)*: sad; gloomy; depressed

mentor (MEN-tawr) *(n)*: a trusted adviser or teacher

mercurial (mer-KYOOR-ee-uhl) *(adj)*: quick; active; eloquent; clever

metabolism (muh-TA-buh-lih-zuhm) *(n)*: the chemical changes within a body, the buildup and breakdown of substances (often specifically used to refer to the breakdown of food and its transformation into energy)

microchip (MY-kroh-chip) *(n)*: a tiny electronic circuit used to process information, as in a computer or calculator

microscope (MY-kruh-skohp) *(n)*: an instrument for viewing tiny objects

microscopic (mie-kruh-SKAH-pik) *(adj)*: requiring a microscope to be seen; tiny

mogul (MOH-guhl) *(n)*: A very wealthy or powerful person, especially a businessperson

monarch (MAH-nerk) *(n)*: the ruler of a state, such as a king or queen

monopolize (muh-NAH-puh-lize) *(v)*: to take control of; dominate

monopoly (muh-NAH-puh-lee) *(n)*: control of a product or service by one person or company

monotonous (muh-NAH-tuh-nuhs) *(adj)*: continuing in the same tone; not varying

monsoon (mon-SOON) *(n)*: a seasonal wind of the Indian Ocean and southern Asia

mourn (mawrn) *(v)*: to feel or express sorrow for

multitask (MUHL-tee-task) *(v)*: to perform two or more tasks at the same time

multitude (MUHL-ti-tood) *(n)*: a great number

mummification (muhm-uh-fah-KAY-shun) *(n)*: the process of treating a dead body with chemicals and wrapping it linen to preserve it

muscular (MUHS-kyuh-ler) *(adj)*: of, relating to, or consisting of muscle

mutually (MYOO-choo-uhl-ee) *(adv)*: equally; jointly

N

nanosecond (NAN-uh-sek-uhnd) *(n)*: one billionth of a second

nicotine (NIK-uh-teen) *(n)*: a poisonous substance found in tobacco leaves, roots, and seeds

nonessential (non-uh-SEN-shuhl) *(adj)*: not essential; unnecessary

nonstop (NON-STOP) *(adv, adj)*: without a stop; not stopping

O

objective (uhb-JEK-tiv) *(adj)*: without bias or prejudice, not affected by personal feelings

objective (uhb-JEK-tiv) *(n)*: a goal or aim

odyssey (OD-uh-see) *(n)*: a long series of wanderings or travels

outlet (OUT-let) *(n)*: a means of expression; an opening or passage; a receptacle into which an electric plug can be inserted to connect with a power supply

overconfident (OH-ver-KON-fi-duhnt) *(adj)*: too confident or sure of oneself

overcrowded (OH-ver-KROU-did) *(adj)*: too crowded

overdue (oh-ver-DOO) *(adj)*: past the time due or expected

P

parallel (PAR-uh-lel) *(adj)*: extending in the same direction, at the same distance apart, so as never to meet

paraphrase (PAR-uh-fraze) *(v)*: to restate in another way

parasite (PAR-uh-site) *(n)*: an animal or plant living on another

pasteurize (PAS-chuh-rize) *(v)*: to heat to a high temperature for a set period of time in order to destroy bacteria

pending (PEN-ding) *(adj)*: not yet decided

perimeter (puh-RIH-meh-ter) *(n)*: the outer boundary of an area

periscope (PER-uh-skohp) *(n)*: an instrument for viewing objects not directly in the viewer's line of sight

persistent (per-SIS-tuhnt) *(adj)*: not giving up; determined

persuasion (per-SWAY-zhuhn) *(n)*: ability to persuade; convincing through the use of argument

pescatarian (PES-kuh-TAHR-ee-uhn) *(n)*: a vegetarian who eats fish

petrified (PE-truh-fide) *(adj)*: turned into stone or a substance of stonelike hardness

pharaoh (FAIR-oh) *(n)*: a ruler of ancient Egypt

phonetic (fuh-NEH-tik) *(adj)*: relating to or representing speech sounds

phonograph (FOH-nuh-graf) *(n)*: an instrument for reproducing recorded sounds

picturesque (pik-chuh-RESK) *(adj)*: visually pleasing or charming

pixel (PIK-suhl) *(n)*: one of the tiny picture elements that together make up the image displayed on a video screen

plutocracy (ploo-TOK-ruh-see) *(n)*: rule by the wealthy

pod (pod) *(n)*: a small group of animals, such as seals or whales

portfolio (pawrt-FOH-lee-oh) *(n)*: a flat, portable case for carrying papers, drawings, or photos

precede (pri-SEED) *(v)*: to go or come before

predict (pri-DIKT) *(v)*: to say in advance; tell ahead of time (literally, "to say before")

predictive (pri-DIK-tiv) *(adj)*: likely to predict

prejudice (PREJ-uh-dis) *(n)*: judgment or opinion formed beforehand

preoccupied (pree-OK-yuh-pide) *(adj)*: lost in thought

prequel (PREE-kwuhl) *(n)*: a movie or literary work about events that occur before those in another movie or work

preventive (prih-VEN-tiv) *(adj)*: devoted to or concerned with prevention, the avoidance of something (in medicine, specifically of disease)

primitive (PRIHM-mi-tiv) *(adj)*: not advanced; simple; crude

profile (PROH-file) *(n)*: a side view, especially of a human face or head; a short, biographical description of a person

prominent (PRAHM-muh-nuhnt) *(adj)*: standing out; noticeable; conspicuous

propel (pruh-PEL) *(v)*: to move forward

puny (PYOO-nee) *(adj)*: lacking in size, power, or importance; weak

pursue (per-SOO) *(v)*: to follow, especially in an attempt to reach a goal or result

R

recall (ri-KAWL) *(v)*: to bring back to mind; remember; to request or order the return (of a product) to the manufacturer

recreation (rek-ree-AY-shuhn) *(n)*: any form of play or amusement intended for relaxation or refreshment

reluctant (ri-LUHK-tuhnt) *(adj)*: hesitant

rendezvous (RAHN-day-voo) *(n)*: an appointment to meet at a set place or time

representation (rep-ri-zen-TAY-shuhn) *(n)*: an image; likeness

retain (ri-TAYN) *(v)*: to continue to have or hold; keep; to employ by paying a fee; hire

ritzy (RIT-see) *(adj)*: From the Ritz hotels, known for their showy style and luxuriousness

S

satisfactory (sat-is-FAK-tuh-ree) *(adj)*: able to fulfill a need, requirement, or demand; acceptable

scribe (skrahyb) *(n)*: a person whose job is to write down information

secrecy (SEE-kruh-see) *(n)*: condition of being secret

sentimental (sen-tuh-MEN-tl) *(adj)*: having or showing tender feeling; influenced by emotion rather than reason

sentinel (SEN-tn-l) *(n)*: a person who stands guard or keeps watch

shortage (SHAWR-tij) *(n)*: condition of not having enough; lack

shrewd (shrood) *(adj)*: clever; sharp

significant (sig-NIH-fi-kuhnt) *(adj)*: worthy of note; important

simplify (SIM-pluh-fie) *(v)*: to make simple

solely (SOHL-lee) *(adv)*: not including anything else

specific (spi-SIF-ik) *(adj)*: clearly expressed; precise; particular

spectator (SPEK-tay-ter) *(n)*: a person who sees or watches

speculate (SPEK-yuh-layt) *(v)*: to think about the possibilities; ponder; consider

stamina (STAM-uh-nuh) *(n)*: endurance or staying power; the ability to last through a stressful effort or activity

standardize (STAN-der-dize) *(v)*: to make standard

subjective (suhb-JEK-tiv) *(adj)*: affected by personal feelings, experience, or background

suite (sweet) *(n)*: a group of connected rooms making up one unit

summon (SUHM-uhn) *(v)*: to order to come; call for

supervise (SOO-per-vize) *(v)*: to oversee or manage

symphony (SIM-fuh-nee) *(n)*: a musical composition for an orchestra

T

tariff (TAR-if) *(n)*: a government tax on imports or exports

testify (TES-tuh-fie) *(v)*: to make statements sworn to be true in a court of law

theatrical (thee-A-tri-kuhl) *(adj)*: of or relating to the theater

theology (thee-AH-luh-jee) *(n)*: the study of religious faith

treacherous (TREH-cher-uhs) *(adj)*: dangerous; hazardous

triumphantly (try-UHM-fuhnt-lee) *(adv)*: in a victorious way

tundra (TUHN-druh) *(n)*: vast, treeless plain of the arctic regions

turbulent (TUR-byuh-luhnt) *(adj)*: characterized by violent motion

tycoon (tie-KOON) *(n)*: a wealthy and powerful businessperson

U

unanimously (yoo-NAN-uh-muhs-lee) *(adv)*: with the agreement of all

unforeseen (uhn-fawr-SEEN) *(adj)*: not expected

unify (YOO-nuh-fie) *(v)*: to combine into one; bring together; unite

unison (YOO-nuh-suhn) *(n)*: in agreement or at the same time

unite (yoo-NITE) *(v)*: to combine to form one; join together

unity (YOO-ni-tee) *(n)*: condition of being one, or united

universal (yoo-nuh-VUR-suhl) *(adj)*: included or occurring everywhere

unravel (uhn-RA-vuhl) *(v)*: to come apart as a result of threads separating

V

valiant (VAL-yuhnt) *(adj)*: brave; bold; courageous

virus (VIE-ruhs) *(n)*: a usually destructive computer program that produces copies of itself and inserts them into other programs without the user's knowledge

visibly (VIZ-uh-bulee) *(adv)*: in a visible way; so as can be seen

visual (VIH-zhuh-wohl) *(adj)*: related to seeing

volt (vohlt) *(n)*: a unit for measuring electrical power

W

warrant (WAWR-uhnt) *(v)*: to serve as reason for; justify; call for

westward (WEST-werd) *(adv)*: toward the west

withdraw (with-DRAW) *(v)*: to take back; remove

withstand (with-STAND) *(v)*: to oppose or resist; stand up against

Z

zeal (zeel) *(n)*: eagerness and excitement about something

Index

A

Abstract nouns, 33
Activities
  Abstract Exhibit, 33
  Accept or Reject?, 114, 198
  Act Out in Class, 8–9
  Ad Campaign, 216–217
  All About Us, 32–33
  Alliteration Nonsense, 23
  All My Friends Say . . . , 48
  In All Seriousness, 220
  Asked and Answered, 126
  Ask Me Again, 126–127
  Been There, Done That, 148
  Belittled in Boston, 19
  Box It, 191–196
  Brave New World, 133
  Break It Up!, 77
  Business or Pleasure?, 49
  But Wait! That's Not All, 204
  Can You Picture This?, 49
  Career Paths, 118
  Clue Review, 169
  Compact = *Kompakt*, 203
  Compare and Contrast, 66
  Connotations, 208–211
  Copycat, 132
  Crystal Ball, 119
  Curious George, 168
  Devil's Advocate, 225
  Did You Know?, 16
  Did you Know?, 56–57
  Disc Jockey, 82

  Divide and Conquer, 183–184
  Do the Math, 132
  Draw It!, 59–60
  Eavesdrop, 168
  Eeny Meeny Miney Moe, 218–219
  E-Game, 109
  Encore! Encore!, 225
  English Without Borders, 110
  Environmental Print, 224–225
  Exploring Key Words, 72–74
  Family Reunion, 65
  A Few Questions, 178–179
  Figurative Trading Cards, 184–185
  Five-Minute Mastery, 189
  Follow the Clues, 151
  Follow the Leader, 109
  Food Me Once, 83
  Game Show, 162
  Give It a Day, 180
  Goods and Services, 37
  Have a Conversation, 115
  Have You Ever. . . , 56, 77–78
  Here I Am, World, 203
  I Can Explain, 158–161
  If You Wrote the News, 78
  I Have a Dream, 224
  Improving Sentences, 9–10
  I'm Thinking of a Word. . . , 199
  I'm Watching You, 216
  Is a Cookie *una galleta?*, 133

  It's All in Your Head, 18–19, 104–105
  It's Greek to Me, 169
  Just a Little Thing, 65
  Just Say It!, 12
  Let Me Explain, 36–37
  Let's Disagree, 224
  Let's Get Jiggy, 23
  Letter to the Editor, 13
  Literal or Figurative?, 185
  Long Arm of the Law, 129
  Look It Up!, 103–104
  Me, Myself, and I, 74–75, 174–175
  Memory Game, 23–24
  A Mile in Your Shoes, 146–147
  Misbehaving with Words, 24
  Mix and Match, 128
  Mock Trial, 133
  Move Pitch, 65–66
  Movie Poster, 44
  Multiple-Meaning Mixer, 174
  My Eponym, 109
  My Fellow Classmate, 158
  My Follow Mammal, 157
  My Own Personal Context, 168
  Need an Alibi?, 128–129
  New Contexts, 162
  In the News, 48
  Notice Me!, 23
  Now and Later, 15, 92
  The One and Only—Or Not, 204
  One of a Kind—or One of Many?, 110
  In Other Words, 48, 219

Activities (continued)
    Parlez-vous français?
        ¿Hablas español?,
        24
    Passion Club, 199
    Person, Place, or Thing?,
        40–41, 152–153
    Pick One, 41
    Pick Three, 90
    Play Me a Tune, 203
    Popcorn and Movies,
        211–212
    Prefix Matchup, 14–15
    Prefix Wheels, 6–8
    ¡Que Misterioso!, 83
    Rhythm, 12
    Rock My World, 133
    Root Canal, 65
    On Second Thought, 204
    Seek and Find, 163
    Sensory Appeal, 88–89
    Set Me Free-In Verse!,
        196–197
    Share and Compare,
        145–146
    Show-and-Tell, 132
    Sling Some Slang,
        168–169
    Smart Aleck, 48
    Song in My Heart, 204
    So You Want To . . . , 105
    Spare Change, 82–83
    Spin the Bottle, 188–189
    Suffix Matchup, 39–40
    Suffix Organizers, 30–32
    Suffix Wheels, 35–36
    A Suitcase Full of
        Words, 133
    The Survey Says. . . ,
        169
    Talking in Class, 18
    Telling Stories, 110
    Tell Me!, 49
    Tell Me About It, 180
    There, They're, or Their,
        204
    Think Fast, 92

    Thinking of You,
        114–115
    This Was Then. This Is
        Now, 101
    Time Capsule, 44–45
    Tinker with It, 65
    10 Things I Love About
        You, 196
    Tongue Twisters, 66
    Track Five, 169
    Two Sides of the Coin,
        186–188
    Unite and Party, 24
    Visiting Celebrity,
        100–101
    Wanted: YOU!, 175–176
    Weekend Theater
        Review, 43–44
    Welcome to My World,
        61, 211
    What Did You Just Say!,
        225
    What Happens Next?,
        153–156
    What's a Newbery, 82
    When I Grow Up, 66
    Where in the World?,
        89–90
    Word Associations, 109
    Word Doctor, 225
    Word Pairs, 214–215
    Wordplay, 224
    Word Problems, 75
    The Write Stuff, 83
    Yellow Pages, 110
    Yes, It Is—No It's Not,
        95–100, 120–125
    You and Your Bling, 117
    You Be the Teacher,
        55–56
    You Crack Me Up, 82
    Your Choice, 92–93
    Your Pixels Are
        Showing, 132
    Your Turn to Teach, 61
    You Take the Cake, 203
Adjective, defined, 28

Adjective suffixes, words
    with, 38
Adverb, defined, 28
Adverb suffixes, words
    with, 42–43
Anglo-Saxon prefixes,
    words with,
    16–17
Antonyms, 142, 191–196

B

Base word
    adding prefixes to com-
        mon, 11
    defined, 2, 20
Base words, adding suf-
        fixes to
    that end in y, 69
    that end with a silent e,
        70

C

Character, words that de-
        scribe, 197
Comparisons, looking for,
    141
Concise Oxford English
    Dictionary, 228
Connotations, 207, 220
    words with positive and
        negative, 207–208
Context
    defined, 136
    learning words from,
        135–139
Context clues, using,
    136–142
    comparisons, 141
    contrasts, 142
    descriptive details,
        137–138
    examples, 139–140
    explanations or defini-
        tions, 138–139
    synonyms, 140
Contrasts, looking for, 142

D

Definitions, looking for, 138–139
Denotation, 207, 220
Descriptive details, examining, 137–138
Descriptive words
  that describe physical characteristics and appearance, 190–191
  using, with specific meanings, 189–190
Details, examining descriptive, 137–138
Diacritical marks, 227
Dictionaries
  free online, 228
  print, 228
  subscriptions to, 228
  using, 151-152, 227
Dictionary.com, 228

E

ELL Activities
  Compact = *Kompakt*, 203
  Compare and Contrast, 66
  English Without Borders, 110
  Is a Cookie *una galleta?*, 133
  It's Greek to Me, 169
  In Other Words, 48
  Parlez-vous français? ¿Hablas español?, 24
  What Did You Just Say!, 225
English language
  borrowing words from, 91
  expansion of, 112
Eponyms, 101

Etymology, 109
Examples, looking for, 139–140
Explanations, looking for, 138–139

F

Fake words, 83
Feelings, words with, 206–207
Fiction text
  reading a, 148–150
  words from a, 150–151
Figurative language, 180–183, 185–186
  hyperbole as, 181
  irony as, 182
  metaphors as, 181
  personification as, 182
  similes as, 181
Foreign languages, words from, 86–88, 90–91
Formal words, 217–218
Free online dictionaries, 228

G

Greek prefixes, words with, 13–14
Greek roots, words with, 54–55, 61–62

H

History text
  reading a, 159–161
  words from a, 161
Homographs, 204
Homonyms, 204
Homophones, 204
Hyperbole, 181

I

Idioms, 203
Irony, 182

J

Japanese language, words from English in, 91

L

Language. *See also* English language; Foreign languages expansion of, 112
Latin prefixes, words with, 5–6, 10–11
Latin roots, words with, 57–58
Legal words, 127
Literal uses of words, 180–183, 185–186

M

Meaning, understanding shades of, 205–225
Medical words, 119–120
Merriam-Webster English Dictionary, 228
Merriam-Webster Online, 228
Merriam-Webster Unabridged Dictionary, 228
Messages, words with, 212–213
Metaphors, 181
Mood, words that describe, 197
Multiple parts, words with, 71–72
Mythology, words from, 86, 91–92

N

Narrative process, 154
Nonfiction text
  reading a, 143–144
  words from, 144–145
Nouns
  abstract, 33
  defined, 28

Nouns (continued)
words from proper, 86,
101–102
Noun suffixes, words with,
29–30

O

Oxford English Dictionary,
228

P

Parts, words with multiple,
71–72, 76
Parts of speech
adjective as, 28
adverb as, 28
checking dictionary for,
151–152, 227
noun as, 28
suffixes and, 29, 45
verb as, 28
People, words from the
names of, 101–102
Personality, words that describe, 197
Personification, 182
Physical characteristics
and appearance,
words that de-
scribe, 190–191
Places, words from the
names of, 101–102
Prefixes, 1–24
a-, ab-, 5, 20
activities with, 6–10,
12–13, 14–16,
18–19, 23–24
adding, 68–69
be-, 16, 17, 20
bi, 4
com-, con-, 5, 20
de-, 5, 20
defined, 1, 2, 20
dis-, 5, 6, 20
fore-, 16, 17, 20
forming words with,
2–3

forming words with suf-
fixes and, 67–83
in-, 10, 11, 20
meanings of, 4
micro-, 13, 20
mis-, 3
mon-, mono-, 13, 14, 20
multiple, 5
non-, 10, 11, 20
over-, 16, 17, 20
para-, 13, 14, 20
peri-, 13, 14, 20
pre-, 10, 11, 20
re-, 3
reasons for learning
about, 4
spelling of, 4
uni-, 10, 11, 20
with-, 16, 17, 20
words with Anglo-
Saxon, 16–17
words with Greek, 13–14
words with Latin, 5–6,
10–11
Print dictionaries, 228
Pronunciation, 227
Proper nouns, words from,
86, 101–102

R

Roots, 51–66
activities with, 55–57,
59–61, 65–66
aster, astr, 54, 55, 62
bio, 54, 55, 62
ced, cede, ceed, cess, 57,
62
defined, 2, 20, 51, 52, 62
logy, 54, 55, 62
meanings of, 54, 62
pend, pens, 57, 58, 62
phon, phono, 54, 55, 62
reasons for learning
about, 52–53
scrib, script, 53
spec, spect, 57, 58, 62
spelling of, 54, 62

vid, vis, 57, 58, 62
words with Greek,
54–55, 61–62
words with Latin, 57–58,
62

S

Scanning, 67, 68
Science text
reading a, 154–156
words from a, 156–157
Science words, 115–116
Sentences, improving, 9–10
Similes, 181
Skimming, 67, 68
Sources, learning words
from other,
85–100
Suffixes, 24–49
activities with, 30–33,
35–37, 39–45
adding
to words that end in
silent e, 70
to words that end in
y, 69
-age, 29, 30, 45
-al, 38, 45
-ant, -ent, 38, 45
-ate, 34, 45
-cy, 29, 45
defined, 2, 20, 25, 26, 45
-en, 34, 45
forming words with pre-
fixes and, 67–83
-ful, 26
-fy, 27, 45
-ic, -ical, 38, 39, 45
-ity, -ty, 29, 30, 45
-ive, 38, 39, 45
-ize, 34, 45
-ly, 42, 45
meanings of, 28, 45
-ment, 27
-ness, 29, 30, 45
parts of speech and, 29,
45

reasons for learning
    about, 27–28
spelling of, 29, 45
-*ty*, 29, 30, 34
-*ward*, 42, 43, 45
-*wise*, 42, 43, 45
words with adjective, 38
words with adverb,
    42–43
words with noun, 29–30
words with verb, 33–34
Synonyms, 191–196
    defined, 140
    looking for, 140

T

Technology words,
    115–116
Tone, words that carry a,
    217

V

Verbs, defined, 28
Verb suffixes, words with,
    33–34

W

Word meanings, 171–204
    descriptive words with
        specific, 189–191,
        197
    figurative, 180–183,
        185–186
    literal, 180–183, 185–186
    shades of, 205–225
    words with multiple,
        172–174, 176–177

Words
    with adjective suffixes,
        38
    with adverb suffixes,
        42–43
    with Anglo-Saxon pre-
        fixes, 16–17
    base, 2, 20
    borrowing from the
        English language,
        91
    describing character,
        197
    describing mood, 197
    describing personality,
        197
    describing physical char-
        acteristics and ap-
        pearance, 190–191
    descriptive, 189–191
    different meanings for,
        171–204
    fake, 83
    with feelings, 206–207
    from a fiction text,
        150–151
    from foreign languages,
        86–88, 90–91
    formal, 217–218
    forming, with prefixes,
        2–3
    forming with prefixes
        and suffixes, 67–83
    with Greek prefixes,
        13–14
    with Greek roots, 54–55,
        61–62

    from a history text, 161
    with Latin prefixes, 5–6,
        10–11
    with Latin roots, 57–58
    learning from context,
        135–139
    learning from other
        sources, 85–110
    learning new and spe-
        cial, 111–133
    legal, 127
    medical, 119–120
    with messages,
        212–213
    messages in, 212–213
    with multiple parts,
        71–72, 76
    from mythology, 86,
        91–92
    from a nonfiction text,
        144–145
    with noun suffixes,
        29–30
    with positive and nega-
        tive connotations,
        207–208
    from proper nouns, 86,
        101–102
    science, 115–116,
        156–157
    technology, 115–116
    that carry a tone, 217
    with verb suffixes,
        33–34

Y

Yourdictionary.com, 228